WALTHAM
MEMORIES

Waltham Library. (By Lewis Willows, Leas Junior School)

WALTHAM
MEMORIES

Jennie Mooney

This book is dedicated to all 'Wattamites' past, present and future.
(A 'Wattamite' has been defined as a long-term resident of the village)

First published 2010

The History Press
The Mill, Brimscombe Port
Stroud, Gloucestershire, GL5 2QG
www.thehistorypress.co.uk

British Library Cataloguing in Publication Data.
A catalogue record for this book is available from the British Library.

ISBN 978 0 7524 5571 6

Typesetting and origination by The History Press
Printed in India by Nutech Print Services

Contents

Acknowledgements

I would like to thank the following people for their contributions to, and support for, this project: Bill and Ray Adams, Cynthia Appleton (*née* Coop), Kath Blyth (*née* Asquith), Simon Balderson, Paul Boag at Proquest, Marjorie Browne, Peter Burns, Janet Clarke, Anne Cook, Derrick Coop, Pete Fowler, Ray and Edith Green, Evelyn Hemmingfield (*née* Briggs), Barry Herbert, Allen Parker, Nellie Peall (*née* Stones), Allan Plastow, Christine Tindall (*née* Coop), Marie Townsend, Barbara West (*née* Stamford), David White, Tom Wood, Dinah and Pete Woodliff, Audrey Wright and the late Philip Wright.

I would like to thank the following people for allowing me to reproduce images from their private collections: Bill and Ray Adams, Kath Blyth, Janet Clarke, Mrs N. Crossland, Evelyn Hemmingfield, Linda Norris, Nellie Peall, Christine Tindall, Marie Townsend, David White, Tom Wood, Colin Wright.

Thanks also to the children of Class 4 (2008/09) Waltham Leas Junior School and their teacher Monica Cross, and to Linda Roberts at the *Grimsby Telegraph*.

Special thanks to my colleagues in Grimsby Reference Library and Waltham Library.

SUPPORTING DOCUMENTS USED IN THIS PUBLICATION:

Census returns: These are available via www.ancestrylibrary.com (hosted by Proquest) in all North East Lincolnshire Council Libraries (except Scartho).

Skelton collection: A collection on microfilm held in Grimsby Reference and Local History Library of items printed by William Skelton of Grimsby between 1824 and 1861. The collection portrays the social history of the town and surrounding villages and includes notices of elections, regattas, religious meetings, auctions and social occasions.

Photographs: The Local History photograph collection consists of nearly 100,000 images of Grimsby, Cleethorpes and the surrounding area, including many rural Lincolnshire villages. It includes approximately 17,000 images put together by Bill Hallgarth dating from the nineteenth and twentieth centuries. The photographs reflect the history and experiences of local people and local ways of life. Some of the images used in this book have been supplied by contributors and are acknowledged accordingly.

Artwork: Local History is incorporated into the National Curriculum at Key Stage 2. Many of us will have seen children from the Leas School as they go on their tours of the village, identifying the older buildings and landmarks. Children from Class 4 produced artwork as a result of what they saw on their tour and these pictures have been used to illustrate the book. Their teacher, Monica Cross, also let me scan copies of the work produced by two pupils who recorded details of their visit to All Saints' Church, Waltham.

Introduction

This book has evolved from an idea I had in the summer of 2008. Having worked with North East Lincolnshire Library Service's Local History photograph collection for many years now, I know that whenever people see photographs of their local area from times gone by, the images evoke a flood of memories. I have attempted to capture some of these memories about Waltham from local residents past and present. Who better to ask about the past than the very people who have lived through it? It must be pointed out that memory is very subjective and recollections of the village and of events may differ from person to person, but this may be regarded as the very essence of living history.

I launched the Waltham Local History Project in September 2008 with publicity sent out via local libraries, schools, Waltham Parish Council, the Church, local groups and the local press. The article in the *Grimsby Telegraph* was seen by people who had grown up in the village but who no longer live locally and they were kind enough to write to me with information. I also received letters and emails from Waltham residents. Others were happy for me to visit them in their homes and to take notes as they reminisced about their lives in the village. We also held two reminiscence sessions at Waltham Library, where people gathered to share their memories with children from Class 4 (2008/09) at the Leas Junior School.

One recurring theme that runs through many of the contributions I received is the sense of community that existed in the village in the twentieth century. Villagers looked out for one another and helped each other out – everybody knew everybody else and there was a strong community spirit. In the space of one generation, Waltham has left behind its image of a rural and agricultural village to become an ever expanding, thriving community with many new inhabitants. I would like to think though that its heart remains the same.

Thanks go to everyone who has contacted me, spoken to me and helped me with this project. This book has been written by the people of Waltham and without you, it would not have been possible. I hope that you enjoy it and that it will be enjoyed by future generations.

Jennie Mooney, MA
Learning and Information Services Librarian

Biographies

Bill Adams: Bill's parents moved to Waltham from Melbourne Avenue in Scartho in 1930 when Bill was born. They owned the bakery in the High Street, on the premises now occupied by the Saddlery.

Kath Blyth (*née* Asquith): Kath came to live in Waltham in 1933 and worked for C.J. Porter Tools Ltd for a total of thirty-six years. She still lives in Waltham with her husband Gordon.

Marjorie Browne: Marjorie came to Waltham with her parents and brother in 1919. She attended the Church of England school in Cheapside and still resides in the village.

Peter Burns: Peter was born in Waltham in 1946 and attended the Methodist school in New Road. A keen artist, Peter donated his painting of the cottage on the corner of Fairway to Waltham Library.

Anne Cook: Anne moved to Waltham in 1947 when she was eleven years old and attended the Church of England school in Cheapside for a time.

Cynthia Appleton, Derrick Coop and Christine Tindall: Derrick and Cynthia (twins) and their sister Christine all have long-established connections with Waltham. Their grandmother lived at the house in Kirkgate which is now the Tilted Barrel. Their father was William (Bill) Coop and their mother was Ethel May Coop (*née* Powell).

Evelyn Mary Hemmingfield (née Briggs): Evelyn Hemmingfield's husband Bob Hemmingfield was the headmaster of the Church of England school in Cheapside. Evelyn lived in the cottage which is now occupied by Shires Restaurant in the High Street and she attended the Methodist school in New Road.

Allen Parker: Allen was born in Waltham in 1934 and has lived in the village all his life apart from two years away in the army.

Nellie Peall (*née* Stones): Nellie has family connections with Waltham going back to the mid-nineteenth century. Her grandmother was born in a cottage on Barnoldby Road in 1854 and Nellie's father, Fred Stones was born in a cottage by Ludgate Hill at the corner of Trail Poke Lane (now Fairway) in 1886.

Allan Plastow: Allan was born in Grimsby in 1928 and attended Waltham village school in the early 1930s. He now lives in Oxfordshire with his wife Jean.

Marie Townsend: Marie was a founding member of the Waltham Ladies Open Group and still resides in Waltham.

Barbara West (*née* Stamford): Barbara was born in Waltham in 1947 and left the village in 1969 when she got married.

David White: David has family connections with Waltham going back into the nineteenth century. His grandfather was the blacksmith in Waltham before handing over the business to Harry Jackson in 1922. Although David now lives in Berkshire, he was contacted by his friend Barry Herbert, who told him about the project.

Tom Wood: Tom was born in Scotland and his family settled in Waltham early in 1945. He lived with his family in Brigsley Road and attended the Church of England school in Cheapside.

Philip Wright: Philip's wife Audrey contacted me when this project was launched. Her late husband Philip had recorded his memories of life in Waltham and she felt that he would have wanted them to be included in this publication. Philip moved to Waltham with his family in 1928 at the age of three and has documented memories of his life in the village.

❧ One ❧

Education and Religion

Are school years the best years of our lives? Some would agree and others not. The contributors in this chapter recall an education system and style of schooling which is a far cry from our schools of today. We hear about extra-curricular activities that included gardening and vegetable growing, but we are also told about the often harsh discipline that existed in the classroom. The school buildings themselves left a lot to be desired: cold winters with no central heating and trips to the outside loos!

The Church of England school was on Cheapside, whilst the Methodist school was on New Road. The latter is still there to this day, but is now a private residence.

Church, whether it was the Methodist church on Cheapside or All Saints' Church, was always at the core of village life, offering not only spiritual sustenance but also a social life for the villagers, which included outings, meetings and church fêtes throughout the year.

Schools: Waltham (mixed and infants) built in 1868 at a cost of nearly £800 on a site given by Dr Parkinson of Ravendale and including tower with clock, it will hold 100 children. Samuel Gosling master. Wesleyan (mixed and infants) built in 1858 at a cost of £724 for 124 children. Ernest E. Peak master.

(Taken from Kelly's Directory of Lincolnshire 1922)

A VISIT TO OUR VILLAGE CHURCH

On the 26th October in the afternoon our class visited a church called 'All Saints'. We went there because of ou history prodject our "Local Area'. When we arrived there we were greated by are local vicar Reverend Shelton.

Outside The church

Firstly Reverend Shelton showed us some stones on the walls of the church. He told us the largest stones oldest. Inside a stone was a trapped fish. On the roof of the church was a cross. There were two crosses but one fell off in the earthquke.

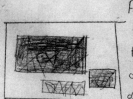

Giving Names

Next Reverend Shelton told us about the font. He said in special services a vicar would christian a baby by putting water on its head. After the baby is christerted its parents would write the baby's name in a speail green book.

Visit to All Saints' Church, Waltham. (By India Taylor, Leas Junior School)

Opposite: *Visit to All Saints' Church, Waltham. (By Pia McLellan, Leas Junior School)*

A Visit To Our Village Church

Our class visited our village
church as part of our class
project on the village. We went
on Monday 20th of October.

Outside the Church

Firstly the vicar, Reverend
Shelton showed us
around the outside
of the church All
Saints Church. Next
we walked around
the building. He quietly said "1420"
he also said during the earthquake
2008 one of the crosses
fell off. In one of the stones
there was a fish trapped. Three
years ago a new roof was
put on.

We all went to Sunday school

When we were younger the church was the main social outlet really, because there was nothing else really, until dad started the youth club. For younger people there was nothing else so we all went to Sunday school, everybody went. It didn't enter into anybody's head whether you wanted to or didn't want to; you went as a matter of course. It was Sunday so you went. In the week there were different things on for the young people, at the church and the chapel, and they ran everything really … I used to go to the keep fit class and swing my clubs.

But it all revolved around the church because there was nothing else and it was too far to go into Grimsby; even when I was younger the buses were only hit and miss, and if it was bad weather, they didn't come as far as us anyway. They stopped at Scartho roundabout. When I was at work, when I was sixteen, around '63/'64 – I used to work at Hainton Square – if it was foggy, often the buses would stop running, and you'd get no warning. Sometimes they would keep going for a while, and if they did they would come to the roundabout (because there was lights that far and there weren't the rest of the way) and I used to walk home from there, in

All Saints' Church, c. 1915. (North East Lincolnshire Council Libraries)

All Saints' Church, 1950s. (North East Lincolnshire Council Libraries)

the dark. You'd hear somebody else walking and never see them. It was the same when it snowed, and it did definitely snow a lot more, a lot heavier and deeper, and the buses would stop. Sometimes they would come as far as Boundary Road and turn round and go back because they had to go up the hill to come into Waltham and then down the High Street and round. We were quite often cut off. It didn't stop us going to school or anything, because the schools were in the village. It's definitely a better bus service now anyway.

Barbara West

The fear of God

I was five years of age when I first attended the Methodist school. My first day will forever stay in my mind. The entire school was assembled to witness the caning and expulsion by the headmaster of three senior boys for some misdemeanour which I cannot recall, although it must have been serious to warrant such a punishment. This put the fear of God into us new pupils which was further enhanced by our teacher, who informed us of the consequences of misbehaving. This teacher was a nasty piece of work who constantly tormented pupils with her bullying and sarcastic remarks. Her first remark to myself being 'who's cut your hair with a basin, your mother?' This set the tone for further sarcastic remarks during the period that she was our teacher.

I remember one poor girl in our class who suffered terribly from boils on both legs which erupted profusely. She was in terrible pain and very distressed. The teacher threatened to punish the girl if she did not stop sobbing. We children felt sorry for her but were unable to help ease her suffering.

Many of the pupils were from less privileged homes and hand-me-down clothes and hobnail boots were common attire. The entrance to the playground sloped upwards and some of the boys would slide down this slope, the hobnails on their boots causing sparks to fly.

During the first year at school we were taught to write on slate tablets before progressing to pencils and then ink dip pens, which were very messy. Of course we had to have an ink monitor to top up the pot inkwells which were inserted into the desktops. These desks would accommodate four pupils and were very ancient. The seats polished from years of bottoms and the tops covered with graffiti – woe betide you if you were caught adding to it, the punishment being a cane across your hands.

In later years we were taught the Marion Richardson method of writing. I became very good at italics, but due to a hand injury in later life I cannot write in longhand.

Peter Burns

A teacher thumped away on the piano and we sang hymns

I was born in Scotland, where my father was a ship surveyor with the old Board of Trade in Glasgow. A lot of his work there was spent ensuring the original *Queen Elizabeth* and *Queen Mary* liners, which were being built on the Clyde, were constructed to the correct specifications and seaworthiness. In 1944, with the country short of food, my father was posted to Hull to get the trawlers that had been minesweeping during the Second World War back to catching fish to help feed a hungry nation. Initially, he moved into digs outside Hull, but after some time his transfer to Hull became permanent and the whole family of my mother, my sister Susan and myself moved to digs in Cottingham, outside Hull. Within months my father was transferred to Grimsby to supervise the return to fishing of Grimsby trawlers and the family crossed over the Humber, initially into digs in Farebrother Street and later St Augustine Avenue.

The Methodist church. (By Bailey Allerton, Leas Junior School)

Early in 1945 my father bought a house in Brigsley Road and we all settled down there. My older sister and myself were sent to the old Church of England school in Cheapside, which oddly enough was next door to the still standing Methodist chapel. Our house in Brigsley Road had been the home of a teacher from the Toll Bar School, who had run the local Home Guard there (and whose name I dare not mention!). We were never too sure what had gone on there as the shed and garden outhouses were full of empty bottles!

Bob Hemmingfield was the headmaster of the C of E school. He came to school every day on a bicycle from his home somewhere off the Barnoldby Road (or was it Fairway?) in Waltham. As far as I can remember, he never had more than two young lady teachers to help him. I can only recall a Miss Timms now, who took charge of the infants. I would imagine there were roughly sixty pupils in the school. I went to the infants, so at playtimes was allowed into the girls' playground. Once you left the infants section the boys then had their own separate playground, where the odd fight was known to break out from time to time! After the 9 o'clock whistle had been blown in both playgrounds, we all lined up and made our way into school where we had prayers. Then a teacher thumped away on the piano and we sang hymns, the words to some of which I can still recall. Once the school registers were taken, we all got down to 'work'. Mr Hemmingfield and his lady assistants were hard-working teachers. However, he was also not afraid to wield the cane for anyone who had misbehaved, though I can't ever recall girls being caned. In keeping with others, I took punishments from him over the years for misbehaving, but only on the palm of the hand in front of the class. It really didn't hurt that much, but was enough to deter you from making the same mistake too often! I never dared tell my parents. You didn't go home and complain of such events in those days or you were asking for even more trouble at home!

The old Victorian school building was 'L' shaped, although there was also a substantial house attached to it on the Kirkgate side, which at one time had been the head teacher's residence. In my day I believe it was occupied by an unconnected

Opposite from top:
Church of England school groups, c. 1928/29. Back row, from left to right: teacher, -?-, Raymond Dawson, Harold Hurst, Dennis Imison, -?-, Spriggy Johnson (son of cobbler). Middle row: -?-, George Parker, Doris Scott, -?-, -?-, Lesley (Les) Wilkinson, Ronald (Ron) Kenny. Front row: two sisters, Gladys Aisthorpe, -?-, -?-, Elsie E. Blakeman, ? Wilkinson, Freda Robinson. (Courtesy of Mrs N. Crossland)

Church of England school groups, c. 1928/29. Back row, from left to right: Harry Leary, Arthur Patterson, -?-, William (Bill) Buffam, Frank Brumpton, -?-, Mr Wilmott (Headmaster). Middle row: -?-, Charlie Alford, Walter (Walt) Harland, Robert (Bob) Fletcher. Front row: -?-, Wilfred (Wilf) Waller, Lesley (Les) Harland. (Courtesy of Mrs N. Crossland)

Johnson family. The infants' part of the school had the only separate room and once you had graduated from the infants there was just one big room with partitions down the centre separating the middle school from the senior school, though not isolating the teachers. In winter there was no central heating; you just put on more clothing, though there was one big coal/coke burning stove in the centre of the larger room. In really cold weather I can remember it sometimes being nearly red hot (what would Health and Safety say today?).

We all got a small bottle of free milk at playtimes in the mornings, but there were no facilities for school dinners and nearly all the pupils went home for their midday meals. I think the few children from Barnoldby-le-Beck who had to walk to school, and walk back after school, past the Waltham brick-pits in Barnoldby road (no school buses in those days), did bring packed lunches.

The school toilets were, to say the least, very basic for boys and not that much better for girls, according to my sister. I can only very rarely remember even the youngest children being accompanied to school by a parent or being met after school – how times change. In the winter, when the roads were covered with ice, the boys used to make slides down the middle of the road (Cheapside) outside the school gates. Traffic was very few and far between, luckily! Opposite the school on the other side of Cheapside was a Temperance Hall, which always seemed shut up during the day, and a few empty houses. Otherwise our boys' playground activities were spent playing 'ciggy' (cigarette cards), marbles and conkers when in season. Outside school hours the highlight of Cheapside was the blacksmith's forge where Mr Jackson carried on his business of shoeing horses and making various metal articles. It was sited almost opposite the current main bus stop. Mr Jackson did not mind too much if passing children popped in to see him at work. In those days Cheapside was a much narrower road than it is today.

I was always very grateful to Mr Hemmingfield for introducing me to soccer and gardening! Every Wednesday (or was it Friday?) afternoon the boys and girls in the senior school were taken in a 'crocodile' down Fairway, then only about half a mile long, and onto the fields beyond, now all built up by the Manor Drive

Opposite from top:
Wesleyan school group, 1927. Back row, from left to right: G. Fidel, Samuel (Sam) Harrison, Mr Barton (Headmaster), F. Smith, Walter Ward. Middle row: -?-, Philip (Phil) Young, R. Lusby, G. Parker. Front row: H. Beacroft, H. Wheeler, Jack Croft, ? Martin, -?-. (Courtesy of Mrs N. Crossland)

Waltham FC, 1950s. Back row, standing from left to right: Frank Parker, Peter Radford, Michael (Mick) McGowan, T. Freeman, Arthur Morris, Ronald Dobbs, P. Banyon (Referee). Middle row: P. Moreley, John Amos, J. Snape. Front row: Ronald Fowler, B. Harrison, Ralph Wilkinson, Norman Markham, B. Cadey. (Courtesy of Mrs N. Crossland)

Estate. I think the girls mostly played rounders there. It was on these fields that I took my first steps at football. We had no football kit and just took off our coats, which became goalposts. Most of us wore quite substantial hobnailed boots to school, which became most effective football boots and, as short trousers were the order of the day (no long trousers for youngsters then), we were ready to play. Mr Hemmingfield was referee. Thus I learnt to play football, an interest which was to stay with me for the rest of my life. It was also through these games that I began to take an interest in the fortunes of Grimsby Town Football Club. This was another activity that has stayed with me through good and bad times, though I never saw a match at Blundell Park until I was ten years old. In those days all young boys supported their local club, not teams from hundreds of miles away with no connection to the area. I am always rather saddened now to see most local youngsters wearing Premiership shirts rather than supporting the local 'Mariners'. We only had one annual competitive football match then. It was against Waltham Wesleyan School. The Wesleyan school was on the corner of New Road and Skinners Lane. It has been a house for many years now. They had the use of a football pitch off Cheapside and I can recall scoring the winning goal there for the C of E boys one year … from centre half!

Another thing about the Methodist school was that next door in New Road was the local barber's shop. Whenever I needed the usual 'short back and sides' my mother would give me four old pennies (2p today) and knotted them up in a handkerchief, so I did not lose them. After school I would take the short cut between houses in Kirkgate that lead into New Road. This was just before Cater's general store and once round the bend, not far off Patchett's large market gardens in New Road. This short cut is still there.

Once a week we had gardening lessons. In those days the road between the school house and the land on the other side of Kirkgate, where it joins Cheapside, was much narrower than it is today. It therefore provided access to a substantial allotment area on the opposite side from the school, where Mr Hemmingfield gave the boys lessons in gardening and growing vegetables. A most useful 'lesson' in the days when food was generally in short supply.

I cannot remember very many of the names of the other boys and girls in my year. There were several members of the quite large and well-known Bennett, Fowler and Hutson families and boys' names, which spring to mind now, were John Enderby, Malcolm Scoffin, Billy Stamford and Brian Snape. Amongst the girls, Brenda Jackson (daughter of the blacksmith in Cheapside) and Joan and Jill Dawson, who caught my eye as being attractive, were all I can recall now. I stayed at the C of E school until 1949 when I won a scholarship (the old Eleven-Plus) to De Aston Grammar School at Market Rasen. It was a good year for passing

The Church school, Cheapside c. 1871. (North East Lincolnshire Council Libraries)

the Eleven-Plus for Mr Hemmingfield as Keith Cook, Alan Graham and Derek Coop (who had a sister called Cynthia) also passed the exam and went on to Clee Grammar School. Children who did not go off to grammar schools went to the Waltham Toll Bar School, then a fraction of the size it is today.

Tom Wood

The children grew vegetables

The Church school allotments were on the corner of Kirkgate and Cheapside and had tall iron gates at the entrance. One afternoon each week was devoted to tending the allotments where the children grew vegetables. We cultivated a good crop of carrots which Mr Hemmingfield then used for the Harvest Festival.

Cynthia Appleton, Derrick Coop and Christine Tindall

Every effort was made to keep us healthy

Over the road that leads to Kirkgate stood the Church of England school. This establishment was larger than the Methodist school situated in New Road, there being much rivalry between the pupils of both schools.

Facing the school stood the Temperance Hall. This was where the pupils of the Methodist school ate our school dinners and those of us that had healthy appetites were always on the lookout for seconds, but you had to be quick off the mark, unless the pudding was frogspawn (as bullet sago was nicknamed), the

An aerial view of Leas School, 1994. (North East Lincolnshire Council Libraries)

supply of which was plentiful due to faddy eaters amongst the girls who disliked its appearance. Any leftover scraps of food were collected for pigswill, no EU regulations back then.

There was a vegetable garden at the rear of the playground – a legacy of wartime necessity – where we were encouraged to plant crops, the garden tools being kept along with the PE equipment in the air-raid shelter, which I think is still there. Every effort was made to keep us healthy in those austere days; sweets were still on ration, but we had plenty of fruit and vegetables and of course free school milk and orange juice. There were not so many faddy eaters then, for if you did not like what was put in front of you it was hard luck for there were no alternatives.

Every year we had a medical examination and, of course, those dreaded jabs when the boys used to tease the girls about the length of the hypodermic needles being used. And of course the Nit Nurse came to the school on a regular basis, ringworm and nits being a common problem and Derback soap being a general item in most households.

A lot of school milk was wasted through over-supply and during the winter months the bottles froze and the cardboard tops were pierced by the birds pecking through them to reach the cream on top of the milk. If you were a milk monitor you were glad to get back in the classroom and warm yourselves by the coke stove. Coke monitor was also another job. Filling the large coke scuttles and carrying them into the classroom needed two pairs of hands.

Way back then Britain was still very patriotic. Empire Day was celebrated, as was St George's Day and of course we had the Queen's Coronation, with every child being presented with a mug and a copy of the New Testament. I still possess the ones presented to me.

May Day was also celebrated and I can recall a maypole being erected in the playground and all the children dancing around it and the May Queen being crowned. Singing and dancing were encouraged and we were even taught Morris dancing. Physical Education was also a priority, with both boys and girls doing exercises in the playground.

Peter Burns

Methodist School Group. Back row, from left to right: ? Beacroft, Ron Lusby, George Fidel, -?-, ? Smith, Sam Harrison, -?-. Middle row: -?-, -?-, -?-, Ethel Kendall, Mary Dalton, Evelyn Briggs, Eileen Fidel, Amy Dobbs, -?-. Front row: Mary Peak, Jack Croft, Phil Young, George Parker, -?-, ? Enderby, Rene Baxter. (Courtesy of Mrs E. Hemmingfield)

I was four years old

I was born in Grimsby 1928, my wife Jean in Cleethorpes also 1928. I started school at Waltham village school in 1932 in the following circumstances. We lived in a small house in Church Lane, with no internal water system; we drew our water via a pump in the garden. At the bottom of the small back garden was a dry stone wall, very roughly built. I was four years old and found that I could climb up this rough wall and on the other side was the school playground. This climb was repeated several times and led to conversations with other children during playtimes.

The playground itself was slightly lower than our garden and I was able to climb down into the playground to join with other children in usual games. My playmates were able to help me back and this became a regular feature. I have a feeling that mother was not aware of what I was doing. After a while it became much easier climbing backwards and forwards. Predictably, one day the headmaster came round to see mother and said my regular escapades were too dangerous to be allowed to continue and suggested that I should be allowed to start school properly – even though under traditional starting age – and enter the school safely.

Another hair-raising incident in Church Lane around about the same time was when the older boys discovered a wasps' nest in the hedge. They were stood around the hedge talking about how to get rid of it. Not being familiar with wasps I decided to show them how, reached into the hedge and pulled the nest down. I think my screams could be heard all over Waltham as the wasps took their revenge. Father rushed me round to the village chemist named Byron Turner. Mother was so impressed with the name Byron that she named my newly born brother Byron.

Allan Plastow

Health and Safety regulations did not apply back then

During playtime, from spring until autumn, girls entertained themselves with skipping, either solo or in threes and fours, or huddled together in groups talking about girly subjects. Boys played marbles or swapped fag cards and football cards, also the cards from PG tea packets and chatted about Meccano and Hornby trains.

We did not seem to take much interest in the girls, although one of the older boys might enlighten us with snippets of information regarding the female anatomy. Sex was taboo and if you were caught fumbling with a girl you received a good hiding both at school and also when your parents were informed by the headmaster. Parents were reluctant to discuss the facts of life, so what you learnt was from the toilet block.

Church Lane (date unknown). (North East Lincolnshire Council Libraries)

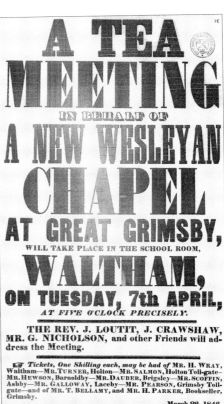

A TEA MEETING

IN BEHALF OF

A NEW WESLEYAN CHAPEL

AT GREAT GRIMSBY,

WILL TAKE PLACE IN THE SCHOOL ROOM,

WALTHAM,

ON TUESDAY, 7th APRIL,

AT FIVE O'CLOCK PRECISELY.

THE REV. J. LOUTIT, J. CRAWSHAW, MR. G. NICHOLSON, and other Friends will address the Meeting.

☞ *Tickets, One Shilling each, may be had of* MR. H. WRAY, Waltham—MR. TURNER, Holton—MR. SALMON, Holton Toll-gate—MR. HEWSON, Barnoldby—MR. DAUBER, Brigsley—MR. SCOFFIN, Ashby—MR. GALLOWAY, Laceby—MR. PEARSON, Grimsby Toll-gate—and of MR. T. BELLAMY, and MR. H. PARKER, Bookseller, Grimsby.

March 26, 1846.

A notice for a tea meeting, 1846. (Skelton Collection, North East Lincolnshire Council Libraries)

Autumn came and conkers were all the rage, with groups of boys searching for them on the way to and from school. Health and Safety regulations did not apply back then.

Latterly, when Mr Thomas Jeremiah had taken over as headmaster from Mr Evans, flush toilets were installed. These replaced the old box closets which had a large bucket underneath the seat which comprised of a wooden plank with three holes. These buckets were emptied on a regular basis by the night soil men who frequently spilt some of the contents onto the playground during this process. During the hot weather we did not hang around that corner of the playground for the smell, combined with that which drifted over from the Tannery in Skinners Lane, became overpowering. Unless one was desperate you hung on until home was reached, not easy on a regular diet of fruit and vegetables.

Peter Burns

My dad used to run the youth club

I went to the Methodist school; both of my brothers went to this school and my mum. After it was finished as a school they used it as a youth club, my dad [Bill Stamford] used to run the youth club in the village from the beginning of the sixties until around 1966. He ran the Army Cadets at the time as well, which was further down the road in a Nissen hut. The kids in the village were getting into a bit of bother – not the kind of bother they get into these days – and so he decided he would do something about it, and he asked the Council if he could use the school because it was empty and going derelict and so they said yes. So he got a load of youngsters from the village and they painted it up inside and out. One young lad painted a mural on one wall and it was absolutely brilliant. It was a shame as they pulled it down eventually.

On the other side of the road was the Temperance Hall, and another hall, and I used to go to them all. I went to church in the night time, I had chapel in the morning and we went to the Temperance Hall for film shows and all sorts of things, it was nice and it was a nice building.

When my mother was at school they used to take the Christmas pudding and a Christmas cake down the baker's shop in the High Street in a big bowl, two of them, her and my friend's mother, and put it in their oven to be cooked. Not long before she died she was telling us that they used to take the cover off the top and pick the currants out whilst walking round.

The house on the corner is supposed to be haunted. Loads of people have said about different ghostly goings-on there. I think it's called the White House.

Barbara West

A silly basket!

Non attendance at school was swiftly dealt with by the appropriately named Mr Goodlad, the local educational attendance officer, who would soon be visiting your parents to enquire the nature of your absence.

Mr Jeremiah encouraged the boys to play football and obtained permission for us to practice in the field at the corner of Skinners Lane and Ings Lane where Alec Archer kept his cows. This field, now built on, was full of humps and bumps and of course cow pats – falling over was not a pleasant experience! He also introduced the boys to the Irish game of Shinty. We were issued with long knobbly sticks with

A notice for sermons, 1854. (Skelton Collection, North East Lincolnshire Council Libraries)

WALTHAM. J.

which the boys delighted in whacking the cow pats – this gave the game a new nickname amongst the boys!

In his wisdom, he had climbing apparatus installed in the playground, which was fastened to the wall of the air-raid shelter. I was the first victim to fall foul of this dangerous equipment, there being no safety surface beneath it so when I fell (or was I pushed?) from the narrow walkway plank I hit my head on the concrete below. This caused concussion and a large swelling the size of an egg to my head. Sent home without hospital treatment, my mother took me to see Dr Fisher who in his Scots vernacular language, called the headmaster a silly basket! Needless to say I soon recovered from my injuries, and following this incident a coconut matting was placed beneath the climbing frame.

I was less fortunate at a later date. The year was 1956 and I was crossing the road from Church Lane after leaving school. I was struck down by a motor scooter, suffering a fractured skull and a broken jaw. This caused me to lose months of schooling and during this period the headmaster organised a collection of books and games from the other pupils to lift my spirits. However, as I began to recover, homework was forwarded on to me and this enabled me to prepare for the Eleven-Plus examination, which I passed with high marks. Unfortunately, I was not selected for the Grammar School. This came as a bitter blow as a lot of my friends with fathers with high status jobs were accepted. I will gloss over what happened next only to say that it was a very unhappy period in my life, although fond memories of the village school linger on.

The little building adjacent to the school, which is now a residence, was at one time a barber's shop.

Peter Burns

Now a residential property

The Methodist school in New Road is now a residential property called School House, but it still has an air-raid shelter in the garden. The Church school was on Cheapside. There used to be a tower on the school, but it became unsafe and was removed. The bell from the tower is now at the church in New Waltham and the clock is the clock we can see on All Saints' Church.

Bill Adams

Opposite from top:
All Saints' Church, 1912. (North East Lincolnshire Council Libraries)

All Saints' Church. (By Francesca Portas, Leas Junior School)

❧ Two ❧

Village Life

This collection of memories recalls the days when Waltham was a truly rural village. Life moved at a much slower pace; milk was delivered by horse and cart in large churns, the village smithy was well known in his place of work down Cheapside, the windmill was a working mill and life, one would assume, was much quieter with far less traffic around. With no internet and no mobile phones, communication depended on good old-fashioned face-to-face conversation. Letters were delivered by the village postmaster whose job also included manning the village telephone exchange.

The old King's Head was a popular meeting place, not only for a pint but as a venue for Hiring Fairs for agricultural workers and domestic servants and also the 'premium stallion scheme', which was run from the large yard and stables at the rear of the pub.

In spite of the post-war hardships and meagre times, the sense of community spirit and a carefree but hardworking existence are strands that weave through all of these memories and make them an invaluable record of times gone by.

My brothers used to have studs in their boots

Waltham was a small village when I came to live in Grimsby Road in 1933. There were no street lights from Boundary Road. It was all fields. We could watch Spurn Lighthouse from the bedroom window. My brothers used to have studs in their boots and would wait till dark to go sliding on the road to see the sparks fly.

We would wait for Roy Markham to come with our milk in two large vessels. The milk would go into basins, then the cream would be skimmed off, put in a bottle and shook till it turned into butter. The hens belonging to Briggs' farm at the end of Grimsby Road laid their eggs in the hedges. We were never short of a good breakfast. There was a greengrocer who came with fresh veg and fruit. He would give us any black bananas he had left at the end of the day. We thought that was their colour.

Our postman was quite a strange man, Jack Kendall. He would ride his bike and keep shouting 'Tally Ho' every so often. Mr Croft would come along with a hand barrow full of fresh bread and cakes. He always gave us the broken cakes. Mr Rimmington was a carrier. He came from Brigsley each day to collect stuff people had bought in Grimsby, including furniture. Our doctor, Mr Chidlow, lived opposite the allotments – the house with the green roof. He was always happy with drink but a good doc for all that.

Kath Blyth

Ings Lane was just a lane with no houses

I am now ninety-four and have many memories of the village, as my parents, brother and I left Cleethorpes in 1919 to live in a bungalow called Nordam, near Nordam Corner, where Brigsley and Waltham meet.

In 1920 my brother and I started school at the Church School in Cheapside. The doctor at that time lived opposite the memorial. Dr McKane's house was demolished and the road widened. He ran a red car and once gave us a lift on our long trek home – a red letter day. The car must have been one of a very few owned at Waltham.

I remember the High Street when the King's Head was flush with the road and nearby was the post office where telegrams were received by Mr Kendall on the phone and delivered by hand.

My family moved to Brigsley Road, Waltham about 1921. Ings Lane was just a lane with no houses and a pond near the cemetery where children fished for tiddlers and I once saw a kingfisher. How the village has changed! Fairway was Trail Poke Lane. Church View and Manor Drive were built on the grounds of the Old Hall.

The public transport then was provided by Provincial and one private bus called ADA, run by a Mr Hargreaves, which started opposite the church by the wall of the hall grounds.

I suppose the biggest alteration to the village came with the demolition of the cottages to make room for the shops and car park and this involved the removal

Waltham High Street. This picture comprises a 1920s image overlaid with an image from 2005. (North East Lincolnshire Council Libraries, courtesy of Simon Balderson)

A provincial bus outside the King's Head, c. 1912. (North East Lincolnshire Council Libraries)

of the picturesque building which housed Topliss' shop selling haberdashery as well as groceries. There were two other grocer's shops: Harrison's on the corner of New Road and High Street and Markham's, where the baker's now stands. Oh, of course there was Cater's space now occupied by Tates [Spar].

In Kirkgate there was the house occupied by Mr and Mrs Robinson (now the pub) and on the spot now occupied by the optician's was a cobbler's owned by an Icelandic gentleman who would mend our boots and shoes while we watched. We liked Mr Holgerson.

The Church school was eventually demolished and I believe the clock was rescued and installed in the church. The Methodist school is no more, but the adjoining house occupied by the headmaster, Mr Barton, is still there. The old rectory was demolished and the gardens now house the council offices. The annual fête was held in those grounds.

Marjorie Browne

I remember when the Old Hall was still standing

My own father knew the miller and sometimes he would take me there before it was open to the public. I remember when the Old Hall was still standing as I had a friend that lived next to it in Manor Drive. An old lady was living at the hall in those days. My friend said that the village boys would go along the underground passage from the church and bang on the hall floor to frighten the old lady. I expect the passage is now blocked off.

Janet Clarke

The graceful Lincolnshire farm wagons were built here

In 1928 my family moved from Healing to a house in Barnoldby Road, Waltham, although I was only three years of age at that time, I can clearly remember this event, our belongings being transported in a van drawn by two horses. I was given the honour of sitting at the front between the driver and his mate. I believe this vehicle was owned by Prikes of Healing.

One of my early memories was of milk being delivered by Mr Archer, who came round in a pony and trap. Milk was brought to the door in a container in which hung a half pint and pint measures with which he poured the required amount into mother's jug.

I will try to set down some of what I recall of the village. I will begin at the junction of Station Road and Grimsby Road: the farm house still standing next to the fire station was Briggs farm house. Proceeding along the High Street came the allotments, at the side of which was a row of walnut trees; as boys we used to steal or 'scrump', as we called it. Unfortunately, this was reported to the school head who asked for a show of hands; anyone who had handled the walnuts would have brown stains on their hands. This would result in a severe caning.

The small tiled building at the side of the allotment (which still exists) was where Mr Walter Douglas, the village road sweeper, kept his wheelbarrow and shovels etc.

Almost opposite what is now known as Manor Drive was just an unmade upland coming to a dead end, with only a pair of semi-detached houses, the half-timbered pair still standing. Opposite the allotment was just fields with cattle, and after Manor Drive came Waltham Hall, the home of Sir George Doughty, next was a farmyard and buildings. The farmer, who lived in the house on Church Lane corner, would open the gates and the cattle in the field I mentioned would walk along to the farmyard – all knowing the way. A section of farm wall is adjacent to the Star Shop (now Co-op) and on this site was W.E. Topliss & Son, a general store; most items could be purchased here. This store was on a rise of the High Street known as Ludgate Hill.

Part of the 1901 Census showing Sir George Doughty at Waltham Hall. (Courtesy of Proquest)

Opposite the manor stands All Saints' Church. To the right of the gateway lies the grave of the Revd Horne, a gentleman I well remember. He always made a point of calling on the villagers and he always carried a bag of what he called his 'Sugar Pennies', a round sugar-coated sweet he would hand to any child he met.

On the corner of Kirkgate was Harrison's Stores, and on the site now occupied by Tates [Spar] was Cator's Stores. There was also Well Lane, the open stream and another shop I remember as a fish and chip shop.

In the cottage almost next door lived an old lady known as Granny Lawrence, always dressed in long black clothing. She rarely spoke and was known by some as the Waltham Witch.

The Church school was at the corner of Cheapside; Mr Willmot was the head – a strict one for discipline. Opposite, on a raised embankment, was the school garden, then fields and on the site now occupied by the hairdresser's was yet another fish and chip shop. After this closed it was used for a butcher's owned by Riley brothers. Next was a stable-doored building in which a foreign gentleman had a cobbler's shop and next the house which is now the Tilted Barrel. This was the home of the Days, who were coal merchants; their coal stocks and vehicles were kept at the rear of the premises.

Then came more cottages and, on the corner of the High Street, Markham's Stores. Down the High Street were more cottages and then the vicarage and its gardens running down the hill to the church hall. In the garden of the hall the Revd Holmes made concrete blocks with straw mixed in them; when set, he wheel-barrowed them to Peakes Lane at New Waltham to build the first church. More cottages, the last one, adjacent to the King's Head gateway, was again a fish and chip shop – the frying range was on the outer wall and, being coal fired, made the wall very warm, and it was a favourite place on a cold night for village lads who had bought a halfpence or pennyworth of chips to sit, backs to the wall, to eat them.

I will digress a little and mention that in one of the cottages lived Miss Sally Lancaster who was wheelchair bound. She made little doll mascots for the RAF aircrews who were stationed at Waltham.

Topliss & Son shop, c. 1954. (North East Lincolnshire Council Libraries)

After the cottages was the old King's Head and then came Kendall's post office with two windows, one usually had a cycle in the window as Mr Kendall sold and repaired cycles. Then more cottages, which still exist, and, as mentioned, Mr Flints the chemist, which became Taskers butcher's. Just around the corner, opposite Barnoldby Road, was a large house, both the home and surgery of Dr Chidlow, who I recall did many operations in his surgery that would have to be carried out at the hospital today. This house was demolished and the present house built on the site.

Returning to Ludgate Hill and Topliss & Sons – next door was Wallers the butcher's, adjacent to the shop was their home and just around the corner in Trail Poke Lane (Fairway) was the slaughter house. I well recall after leaving school in an afternoon, elder lads calling out to hurry to Wallers as they were 'pulling in' – this meant that a beast to be killed would have a rope put around its neck and through a ring on the floor all the lads would haul on the rope until the beasts head was at floor level and the butcher dispatched it with a felling axe.

Across the lane is the protected house on the corner of High Street and then an orchard, I fear many apples got 'scrumped'. Next was the stream that ran under the road and a further row of cottages. In the centre of the High Street was a shop – until recently a gents hairdresser's, I remember being both a greengrocer's and cobbler's.

Swags and Tails was a pair of semi-detached houses; in one lived Mrs Callan, a local councillor, and at the rear of the now dress shop [now Deli] was Mr Croft's bakery. He delivered bread on a hand cart. The next two houses are still occupied and the Do It Yourself shop [now flooring shop] was a bungalow, the home of Mr Howsom, a haulage contractor – his vehicles being kept at the rear. Next was Watkinson's poultry farm; they lived in a wooden bungalow on the site and had tennis courts.

The detached house that comes next was lived in by, I believe, a family named Norwell who had connections with the chapel, and on summer evenings would park a large van on the grass verge, dropping down a screen at the rear and would show a silent movie and hold a collection after the show. I saw my first ever film here, *The Hunchback of Notre Dame*.

Next was Harrison's animal feed mill, driven by a large gas engine. As boys we delighted to see Mr Harrison hang on the huge flywheel to set the machine rolling. Then came fields and Woods farm house (which is still occupied) and then only fields up to Bradley Road.

Across Barnoldby Road was Mr Allison's (the local builder's) clay pits and brick work. Clay dug from the pit was manufactured into bricks; after standing on racks to dry, they had to be baked or burnt in a kiln situated at the road side and was in the charge of Mr Grantham. Also sited here was two cottages occupied by Allison's employees. Towards the village all was open ground, and next came Laburnum Avenue and where Ross Hall now stands came Mr Thornton's wheelwrights, the graceful Lincolnshire farm wagons were built here and the beautiful spoked wagon wheels.

A row of houses and then Mr Portas the newsagents and stores, now known as the Cabin and on the Brigsley Road corner, Mr Allison had Waltham's first street light installed – the only one for some time. A little way up Brigsley Road was our famous windmill, owned by the Rodgers family.

Philip Wright
(Submitted by Audrey Wright on behalf of her late husband)

Waltham Ladies Open Group

In the 1940s, after the Second World War, Mrs Geipel, the then vicar's wife, started a 'Young Wives Group'. The meetings were held in the church hall on the High Street near to what is now the King's Head car park.

At the first meeting it was decided to meet every first and third Wednesday in the month and a committee, consisting of a Group Leader, Treasurer, Secretary and six other ladies was formed. Their job was to organise events like talks, demonstrations and outings that would appeal to young mothers who, in the main, were homemakers.

This proved to be a successful format and up to fifty ladies would enjoy an evening out. Subjects ranged from talks on health, education, charities and slide shows on holidays, wildlife and bygones. Demonstrations were very popular, especially cookery (as we usually had a tasting session afterwards), but we also had jewellery making, basket making, Scottish dancing to name a few.

In the lighter evenings theatre trips were arranged, also visits to many of the food factories in the area. All-day trips were not possible because of being home for the children leaving school.

In the 1980s the name was changed to 'Waltham Ladies Open Group' so that ladies of any denominations were able to join us.

Waltham Ladies Group celebrating their fiftieth anniversary in 1999. From left to right: Alma Montgomery, Marie Townsend, -?- and Ella Now. (Courtesy of Mrs M. Townsend)

Waltham Ladies Group. Marie Townsend, group leader, and members of the committee are pictured cutting the cake on the occasion of the group's fortieth anniversary in 1989. (Courtesy of Mrs M. Townsend)

Over the fifty-four years the group were meeting, we held a charity event every summer, raising in excess of £10,000 for as many charities as possible in our area. Sadly, spiralling costs and reduced membership meant we had to finish, but on a brighter note, about sixteen ladies still meet once a month for coffee or lunch out, and we support the 'Women's Refuge' in Grimsby.

Marie Townsend

We used to love going on the train

When my mother went anywhere, or my auntie, when they lived at the Mill, they came back on the train. They got off at Waltham station and they used to send postcards, and they used to get post four or five times a day in those days. And they would send a postcard from Hull in the morning telling my grandad to pick them up at one o'clock at the station and you could rely on the postcard getting there.

Waltham station, 1961. (North East Lincolnshire Council Libraries)

We used to go on the Louth line because my dad's mother and father lived at Louth. Once every other month we went on the steam train, once a month we went on the bus as it must have been more expensive on the train. But we went into Grimsby [to catch the train], so I don't know if Waltham station was still open then, as this was in the 1950s. I expect because it was near the post office at New Waltham it was too far for us to walk ... so we used to go into Grimsby to catch the Louth train. We used to love going on the train, with the steam, it was lovely.

Barbara West

Boy, what a smell!

As a child we would shop at the many shops in our village. Harrison's had all you could want. I watched mum sit on an upturned box to give her order. Everything was weighed. Lard and butter came in large pats and had to be cut to weight, patted and wrapped in paper, sugar was also in large vessels. It was so exciting when sweets came off ration, we would go to Adams' and get them weighed out of jars.

The village had so many shops I wonder how we manage with so few with the new homes now. I list those I remember: The Cabin (Portess), Tasker's (butcher), Adams' (baker and grocer), Johnson's wool shop, fish shop (Ann Trevor), post office, Markham's (grocer), Harrison's (grocer), Cater's (greengrocer), Topliss' (grocer and haberdash), Waller's (butcher), Young's (sweets and toffee), Gordon's (chemist), Corden's (florist and fruit), Topliss small shop.

Also we had two cobblers – one in High Street and one next to the Tilted Barrel – and one blacksmith [Jackson] opposite the bus terminus (we watched these people doing shoe repairs and doing horses' shoes – boy, what a smell!). There were three halls – one in the High Street near the King's Head and two in Cheapside –, two churches, three schools, and one barber in New Road.

As children we were always busy, plenty of fields to play in, plenty of interesting people to watch at work; they never sent us away. Our bobby would always stop and talk to us. There were some very important people too: Mr Crampin, trawler owner; Mr Dyer, big name in bread; Mr Browne, artist; Mr Vickers, fish merchant; several skippers and lumpers too; Ann Trevor, a well-known singer.

Our lives were very happy thanks to the people that had time for each other and for the children of Waltham.

Kath Blyth

The apples were stuffed under his jumper

Pat Tierney's orchard was an ideal place to go scrumping, but not an ideal place to get caught. Bill remembers the orchard as being on the land where Ashlea Court Residential Home is now. He would climb over a 6ft gate, but on one occasion the village police sergeant was waiting for him as he came out – the apples were stuffed under his jumper but he got a boot on his backside and lost all the apples.

During the First World War the Waltham Excelsior Band left their instruments in the Tannery buildings for safe keeping. Unfortunately, being in the vicinity of tannic acid, the instruments had virtually rotted away by the time they were retrieved. The band disbanded in 1964 and the instruments went to Toll Bar School.

Bill and Ray Adams

Waltham Cenotaph (date unknown). (North East Lincolnshire Council Libraries)

CENOTAPH   WALTHAM

Opposite from top:
Topliss Shop, early 1900s. (North East Lincolnshire Council Libraries)

The King's Head. (By Paige Lowe, Leas Junior School)

It was all made very cosy and warm

I moved into Waltham in 1947 when I was eleven years old and attended the Church of England school in Cheapside for a short time. One of my acquaintances there was Brenda Jackson, daughter of the local blacksmith.

I well remember the church hall in the High Street, for it was there in 1959 that my husband and I held our wedding reception. I remember many concerts in Ross Hall, which went on for hours and people crowded in.

I knew something of the windmill site, for I used to play in the field there, climbing over the dome-shaped huts there, left from the war.

But my special memory is of the now ice-cream shop and café in the railway carriage on the mill site, for my great-grandma used to live there! She was married

Waltham Windmill, c. 2005. (North East Lincolnshire Council Libraries)

to a fisherman and, when he died, was given one of the fishermen's cottages in Mill Road, Cleethorpes. She later re-married and continued to live there, but when the Council found out she was evicted, because she was no longer a widow and therefore not entitled to one of the cottages.

I've no idea how it came about, but my parents procured for them the empty, shabby railway carriage and I remember helping to paint the inside. It was all made very cosy and warm, with a black wood stove. They lived comfortably there for some years, I believe, until the husband died and she became senile and went to live with her daughter in Cleethorpes.

Anne Cook

Yellowhammers and kingfishers were spotted regularly

Cynthia remembers how the local pig farmers would collect pigswill from residents in Brian Avenue and at Christmas the residents would get a pack of food such as bacon and sausages from the pigs that had been slaughtered.

Derrick recalls how Jack Chapman had a calf that needed fostering and he had been trying to get one of the milking cows to take it on, with no success. His tactic then was to set his dogs on the calf, which resulted in the cow's maternal instinct coming through to protect the calf and bond with it.

It would be a common event to see herds of cows driven up Barnoldby Road and Derrick would often walk to school and see the cows walking along next to him. The cows had names like Daisy, Snowball, Spot, Buttercup and the largest one was called Longshanks. Sometimes there would be a bull in their midst!

Wildlife was plentiful with 'red doctors' [sticklebacks] and newts in the local becks. Yellowhammers and kingfishers were spotted regularly.

Christine and Cynthia would go brambling each autumn, mushrooming, gleaning for corn for the chickens and 'wooding' – kicking all the rotten wood from under the hedgerows to collect for fires. There would be rides on hay carts at harvest time and plenty of mice to catch in the fields and amongst the stooks.

They all remember the 'big pond' and the 'little pond' on the land between what is now Archer Road and Albertine Court.

Each October children would be allowed two weeks off school to go potato picking – this was a regular event if you lived in the countryside. Cynthia picked for Wilkinson's at Cheapside when she was about twelve in the late '40s/early '50s. The children were allowed to take potatoes home and her mother always advised her to pick the biggest as they would make the best chips!

Days out would involve walks over the fields to places such as Bradley Woods, Water Dell and Ravendale Valley. A picnic of jam sandwiches would keep them going.

Villagers would go and pay into the 'slate club' at Blakemans cottages, a sort of Christmas club. The savings book was an air force blue colour. There were cottages where the library is situated now and Derrick remembers a pony and trap crashing into one of the cottages.

The church hall in the High Street was a focal point for the community and was used for Brownies, Guides, Red Cross meetings, wedding receptions and other community groups. Christine recalled how women would sing:

'Any rags any bones any bottles today
There's a big raggajack coming down this way'

Swede wine brought back some humorous memories for Derrick – it was no good for anything other than killing ants. He also remembers that a Mrs H., who lived in Brian Avenue, used to make elderflower wine but on one occasion it exploded, splattering wine all over her kitchen.

Cynthia Appleton, Derrick Coop and Christine Tindall.

Mr Sutton had a traction engine

Mr Sutton had a traction engine which he would hire out for threshing and stacking. The village girls would take the workers some plum bread for their lunches. New children would appear at the school for a short time while the harvest was on, or while particular seasonal jobs were available, and then would disappear when the work was over.

The hunt was a regular sight in Waltham, meeting at the King's Head. They once got a fox down New Road.

Each year there would be outings in the charabanc. The charabanc had long seats and all the children would crowd in. Evelyn belonged to the Scartho Guides and the trip was organised to visit the Scouts who were at Swinhope. The journey was cut short when the charabanc broke down on Ashby top and all the children had to get out and push it up the hill! There was also an annual school trip to London, when the whole school would catch the train at the station in New Waltham.

William Horn lived at the rectory; he wore a straw boater in the summer. Tom Rodgers suffered from ill health and had to use a bath chair.

Evelyn Hemmingfield

High Street with King's Head on the left, c. 1920. (North East Lincolnshire Council Libraries)

We often watched the large farm horses being shod

Coming from school we often watched the large farm horses being shod. At [Mr Jackson's] smithy was a large metal disc with a central hole and the wagon wheels from the wheelwrights would be bowled up the road to have a metal tyre or rim fitted. Having made the rim, the smith heated up the rim in a furnace and the rim was laid on the metal disc, the hub fitting in the central hole. When the correct temperature of the disc was reached it was quickly fitted over the wheel and cooled down with cold water to make it shrink to a tight fit.

Almost opposite the smith was the bus stop – from here one could catch Ada or Provincial buses to Grimsby. I think the cost was four old pence return. Next was the stile that led to Brigsley Road, and the next building I remember was the Temperance Hall.

Opposite was the Church school. It had a tower with a clock and as the tower became unsafe it was dismantled and the clock donated to the church. A row of cottages was opposite and next to the school was the chapel, with its hall opposite. A little farther on was Sutton's steam traction engine and threshing machine shed. The machines would go out to the farms to thresh the stacks of corn, a trailer was towed by one of the machines; in this the men lived if it was too far to reach home. I would like to mention the tan yard and horse slaughterers in Ings Lane.

I must mention Mr Harold Rimmington, with his horse-drawn carrier's cart. He would collect any goods or grocery orders for you in Grimsby and deliver to you in the evening. If you required him to call, one placed a card in the window with a large letter R on it.

That must be about the sum of my memories, but I must mention Waltham Flying Club at the end of Cheapside, opened in the 1930s. Great excitement was aroused by the visit of Sir Alan Cobhams Flying Circus with the wing walkers and parachutists etc. An air service to Hull (Brough) was run until the war came when the RAF took over and Waltham became the home of 100 Squadron.

I think few people are aware that in the club's early days, prior to his enlisting in the RAF, Sqd Leader 'Ginger' Lacey was trained here and became the fighter pilot who shot down more enemy aircraft than any other fighter pilot in the Battle of Britain. I also recall a Whitley bomber from Waltham making a crash landing at the end of Trail Poke Lane early on in the Second World War.

Philip Wright

(Submitted by Audrey Wright on behalf of her late husband)

High Street with King's Head on the left, c. 1920. (North East Lincolnshire Council Libraries)

An aeroplane on a motorbike

My grandmother, Emma Collinson, was born in a cottage on Barnoldby Road in 1854 and my father, Fred Stones, was born in a cottage by Ludgate Hill at the corner of Trail Poke Lane (now Fairway) in 1886. Both attended Waltham Methodist School along with my father's brothers and sisters. I have been told there was then a balcony in the school.

My two brothers also attended this school. I started in 1934 when the infant teachers were Miss Cooling (later Mrs Hall), Mrs Evans and Mr Fleming was headmaster and was also a local preacher. The playing field was almost at the end of Ings Lane, a long walk from the school. I used to get my hair cut at the men's barbers next door to the school and was charged 6d. In Kirkgate there was a cobbler – I believe he was an Icelander.

The shops I remember when at school were Cator's, Harrison's, Markham's, Waller's, Tasker's, the post office, Topliss's had two shops, a fish and chip shop and Adams' and Walker's bakery. As school children we attended the opening of Ross Hall and the consecration of the extension to the cemetery. The Methodist hall was in Cheapside where we held our school concerts. Nearby was the Temperance Hall where the school dentist 'performed'. I had my first tooth out there. The church hall was in the High Street. Sally Lancaster sat in a wheelchair outside her house in High Street chatting to passers-by. A lovely cheerful person.

Waltham Windmill. (By Harry Franklin, Leas Junior School)

A copy of the school report for Nellie Stones, 1936. (Courtesy of Mrs N. Peall (née Stones))

Next term begins 7 SEP 1936

Lindsey County Council Education Committee.

~~METHODIST DAY SCHOOL,~~
WALTHAM, Nr. Grimsby.

Midsummer Examination.   Class *Std I*

Dear Sir (Madam),

I beg to forward *Nellie Stones'* Report in the *1936* Examination, and ask your interest in the same.

Yours faithfully,

J. J. Fleming
(Head Teacher)

ATTENDANCES : Possible No. *134*   Actual No. *123*

SUBJECT.	MARKS POSSIBLE.	MARKS GAINED.	REMARKS.
Reading	10	10	Excellent
Composition *Poetry*	10	10	Excellent
English	20	18	Very Good indeed
Arithmetic	40	32	Very Good indeed
History	20	7	—Only Fairly Good
Geography	20	15	Good
Needlework	—	—	Fairly Good
Writing	10	4	This must improve
Dictation	20	19	Excellent
Nature	20	15	Good
Drawing	20	13	Improvement shown.
Gen. Knowledge	20	18	Excellent
Music	20	9	Good
TOTAL	230	170	

Number in Class *12*   Position in Class *5*

General Remarks :

A satisfactory result. Nellie must however try to be tidier

K. M. Remington.
Class Teacher

My father told me his mother used to put ashes on Ludgate Hill in frosty weather to stop the horses slipping. He also said there were six sails on the windmill but when he was a boy there were only four for years. He would be delighted there are now six again!

I am wondering if anyone has told you about the fancy-dress parade which was held on August Bank Holiday Monday – the first Monday in August then. It was always a very big event. The start of the parade was always Mr Cyril Waller and Mr Ern Fowler. I remember one year they had a bed set up on a motorbike; one was in bed and kept producing a chamber pot. Another year they set up an aeroplane on a motorbike.

The parade started at Ings Lane and went through the village either to Mr Harrison's field on Barnoldby Road or Mr Markhams field on Cheapside. I remember our school being on a float and I was dressed up as a dwarf or gnome. Probably Snow White etc.

Nellie Peall

Mum made her own jam

We spent many hours collecting mushrooms from the fields, now Fairway. Brambles were plentiful too. Mum made her own jam.

My school was the Methodist in New Road. The man that lived next to it kept pigs. We could hear them squeal when they brought them there to kill. You could see them hung up to drain – very upsetting for us young children.

The village had a May Queen – all the girls wanted to be one.

My brothers found the tunnels underground from the hall (next to Co-op) when it was pulled down. There are also some from the then vicarage on the green, through the allotments to Grove House at the top of Ings Lane. Our life changed very quick with the war. All the RAF personnel arrived. Some came to live with us with their wives who were also in the RAF. It was quite frightening to hear the siren based on top of the place next to Topliss' small shop. We went to school for a while with our neighbour. There was once when my mother had to run with a pram for cover into a small wood as a German plane came up Pepper's Hill firing his gun. I think he also went around the terminus.

We watched as the Italian prisoners marched past the house to work on local farms. There was the Land Army across the road from us, now the vets, but it was the infant school for many years.

The winters were very cold. It was a long walk to Toll Bar in deep snow. The boys had to wear short pants till they were twelve. We could reach out of our

Grimsby Road, Waltham, winter 1947. (North East Lincolnshire Council Libraries)

Brigsley Road in the 1940s. (North East Lincolnshire Council Libraries)

bedroom window and break large icicles off the gutters to suck – no worry about germs those days.

When the war ended the billets were taken over with squatters, but the officers' huts the Council converted. We had one of those. They were lovely: one large room, one large bedroom and one small, a kitchen, bathroom, and pantry. Our local coalman delivered our ration of coal once a week. We had to make it last.

Kath Blyth

The milk arrived in large metal churns on a horse-drawn cart

For a short time I was a member of the church choir. There was supposed to be an underground tunnel from the church, under the road outside, which connected with the Waltham Hall/manor house. We never found anything of it in the church and I believe when the village hall was demolished (to make way for the Church Leas Junior School and the surrounding estate in the 1960s) that no evidence of it was found there either, but cannot be certain of this.

There was just one doctor in the village in those pre NHS days. He was Dr Chidlow who lived in a big house in High Street beyond the church. He was another well-known character with something of a reputation, but a good man nonetheless. In the days when the old village hall/manor (once the home of the Doughty family of Grimsby fame and fortune) was still there, the district nurse, Miss Mackerill, and her sister Mrs Mathews were residents for a time. Once, when I badly sliced open the palm of my left hand on a rusty nail, my mother summoned the district nurse at high speed to stop the bleeding. There were no stitches in those days and I still have the long scar of around three inches. The district nurse also occasionally turned up at school to check out our hair for nits! Her sister worked at St Martin's School, off Bargate, in Grimsby.

There was also quite a thriving leather tanning business in the village somewhere in the Skinners Lane area, which I think was connected then with the Kemp family. Some sort of tragedy was supposed to have taken place thereabouts then. My mother would have known about it from village gossip at the Mother's Union or the Women's Institute meetings!

Waltham Windmill was still a working windmill in those immediate post-war years, in the hands of the Rodgers family. Occasionally with a school friend, Billy Stamford, who lived nearby, we would be allowed inside the old mill. It only had four sails then and I think its days as a working mill were already numbered. This was before the Preservation Society took over.

An aerial view of Waltham in the 1970s. (Courtesy of Mr B. Adams)

I would imagine that it is now almost totally forgotten that there was once a garage selling petrol at the lower end of Brigsley Road not far from Robinson's Red Roofs house. There was also a small garage at Norman Corner in Brigsley Road, a short distance from the Rimingtons' house. This family ran a carrier business to Grimsby and Mr Rimington also ran a daily bus service into Grimsby from Ashby-cum-Fenby. For many years our near neighbours in Brigsley Road were the Hockney family, who had the bakery business in Cleethorpes ('Billy the Baker'). Other Brigsley Road people I recall were the Bransons, the Dunns, the Harrisons, the Blanchards, the Smelts (market gardeners), the Turners (typewriters), the Carrs (builders), the Wilkinsons and the Barnoldbys. Mrs Barnoldby was noted for her rather 'strange' fashions in those days. Mr Barnoldby was the head of the water works company in Grimsby. They were all good people and always spoke to me and my sister. I consider I have been fortunate to have known them, and so many other characters, from my boyhood introduction to the village of Waltham, now over sixty years ago.

I really lost touch with much of what happened in the village when I went off to De-Aston school in Market Rasen in 1949, followed by a later college spell and two years of National Service in Cyprus with the RAF, then a move away from the village. By then Waltham was changing, almost unbelievably, into a dormitory village for Grimsby with huge new estates, mainly off both sides of Barnoldby Road and the much extended Fairway.

My other memories of living in Waltham itself date from the early years after the Second World War, when we first moved to Waltham. In Brigsley Road our daily milk delivery was supplied to each household by the Archer family of farmers who were, and still are, very well-known in the village. Every day in those early years the milk arrived in large metal churns on a horse-drawn cart. Housewives put out a series of milk jugs and the milk man (usually a very young Alec Archer then) measured the milk from the churns into the jugs. It was so creamy that my mother used to skim off the cream and make butter from it by shaking it violently in a screw-top bottle. The extra butter was a welcome addition to the tiny weekly butter ration which came via our ration books from Topliss' grocery shop. This quaint little shop stood almost opposite Waltham Rectory with its splendid gardens off High Street. I recall Revd Troop and his wife living there. I believe the last to live there was the Revd Geipel with his wife. The impressive old rectory was tragically demolished, I'm told in the 1960s, together with the old post office, the original King's Head pub and a row of terrace houses in High Street near the pub called Providence Buildings. They made way, rather sadly I think, for the new King's Head development of the site.

Tom Wood

Bombs fell behind what is now Neville Turner Way

Derrick, Cynthia and Christine all remember foil ticker-tape type bits of paper being dropped by aircraft from the sky – possibly a method for foiling the radar systems. It was described as silver paper with an opaque backing.

There were two air-raid shelters in Brian Avenue, but they were not frequently used. The children would be lead sleepily from their beds if there was an air raid and would either take shelter under the table or hide under the stairs. Derrick would not be at all surprised to find their neighbour already under the table too.

The air-raid shelters were brick with a flat roof but were very easily destroyed by children after the war, which makes you wonder how they would have withstood being bombed!

Bombs fell behind what is now Neville Turner Way in what was known as the 'third field' – it had large dips and humps in it – possibly a legacy of the old ridge and furrow method of farming?

Christine Coop with her grandmother, Alice Coop, pictured at the house which is now the Tilted Barrel in Kirkgate. (Courtesy of Mrs C. Tindall)

American servicemen lived in the huts on Ings Lane – Cynthia remembers being with her mother and being offered chocolate by one of the Americans. She recalls that Italian Prisoners of War were housed in the huts on Cheapside in and around Mill View and has fond memories of going to see the 'camp pictures' in the big Nissan hut on Elm Road. Derrick remembers a barricade being built to narrow the road near the church so as to slow down any invading enemies! All three siblings remember standing at the Cenotaph watching the convoys on their way to Binbrook.

Cynthia Appleton, Derrick Coop and Christine Tindall.

I am sure a lot of chaps only went for a yarn

I was born in Waltham in 1934 and have lived in the village ever since, apart from two years in the army [nineteen months in Germany]. In the '30s, '40s and '50s the village had few changes, except the RAF camps in the Second World War. These were mainly down Ings Lane and Cheapside.

My childhood home until marriage in 1960 was No. 3 Donton Lea, Church Lane. This is at the bottom of Church Lane and the view from the front bedroom window overlooked Mumby's farm with only fields right to Louth Road, New Waltham.

Farms in the village were Mumby's, Clayton's (previously Chambers' of the famous shop in Grimsby) at the Grove, Archer's in Grove Lane and Brigsley Road, Cheapside had Markham's (now Golf Club and upmarket housing) Jarvis', Wilkinson's (Firs Farm) Sleight's and Shorts'. Barnoldby Road had Kettelwell, Woods, Kirk and Brockelsby. Just past Bradley Road was Haggis's Farm. At the very bottom of Ings Lane was Vermeersch's – he was from Belgium – and his son. A school friend of mine recently told me it was his dad who got the road surfaced; I can remember when it was just a cinder lane.

My childhood and early youth were spent on the farms and were great times; the Shire horses a particular favourite. A crowning moment was being allowed to take two of Markham's to Harry Jackson the blacksmith to be shod. The smithy was at the top of Cheapside near the Cenotaph and Harry used to make and repair most of the farm implements. There was always plenty of locals in there for a natter. Another great talking shop was Steve Bierley's, the barber's in New Road. I am sure a lot of chaps only went for a yarn because the same ones used to be in when I went.

The village has altered a lot over the years, i.e. the demolition of the rectory and village hall (sheer vandalism). The village hall (home to George Doughty) was opposite the church surrounded by a wall and trees. The trees met the churchyard trees, forming an arch which used to clatter the top deck of the bus. The rectory was where the village green is now and used to house garden parties etc. in the gardens. The vicar was Mr Troop, who enjoyed a pint in the King's Head. Opposite the rectory were the shops of Wallers and Topliss (an attractive shop with bow windows); Wallers (butchers) had a slaughter house at the back of the shop. These two shops would deliver your order, coming round earlier in the week to take the order (no phones or online shopping!). Topliss had the Top Shop near the fire station (now a hairdresser at the mini roundabout at the top of the High Street). Other shops were Adams', High Street Harrison's and Cator's, Kirkgate. Opposite Adams' was Croft the baker, who delivered lovely bread and buns in an enclosed handcart.

The two junior schools were the Church School on Cheapside and the Wesleyan on New Road. You attended until age eleven and then Toll Bar or Grammar. Two well-remembered headmasters were Mr Hemmingfield (Church) and Mr Fleming (Wesleyan).

The war years saw the arrival of the RAF and the local girls had plenty to choose from (my sister married an airman). Mother and my sister helped in the WVS in the Temperance Hall (opposite the chapel); the RAF lads were glad of a bit of social life after the horrors of Ops. Mother said you got to know them real

A view of Waltham High Street taken from the rectory roof (date unknown). (North East Lincolnshire Council Libraries)

Rushby's bus (date unknown). (North East Lincolnshire Council Libraries)

well and suddenly they would be missing and when you asked after them their pals would say they had 'bought it on Ops' (Bombing Raids).

Ross Hall was a popular spot with dances and film show etc. The other hall was the Methodist hall on Cheapside, nearly opposite Skinners Lane end. Next to the hall was Sutton's Yard where he kept steam engines which were used for threshing etc.

Development I have seen has been huge, i.e. all of Ings Lane, Grove Lane, Cheapside, Barnoldby Road (both sides), the huge infill between Fairway and Grimsby Road. In my youth you could walk up all the roads and lanes with only fields to be seen at the back of the roadside houses. I have been part of this infill living since marriage in Danesfield Avenue and now Chestnut Road.

I must mention Cooper's Chip Shop in the High Street near Buck Beck; we would sit on the wall with our penn'orth of chips, delicious! At the back of Adams' shop Pete Spenser, an ex-RAF flight engineer, had a garage. He was real good with us lads when we got our motorbikes.

At this time you knew almost everyone in the village and now, because of the size of the population, this is not possible.

My father was a joiner and wheelwright working for Allisons, the workshop was in New Road next to the church. Mother, up to her marriage in 1916, lived at the Brickyard (now angling club, Barnoldby Road.) where her father was foreman.

In the severe winter of 1947 we were cut off from Grimsby until they managed to cut a way through from Boundary Road for a single-decker bus service to run, the snow was up to the bus windows. You could walk over the hedge tops it was so deep. Much to the joy of we Waltham lads, Toll Bar School closed for seven weeks because they could not get coke for the boilers. One of my brothers was on snow clearing – this was done by shovels and they used to get so far down a road [but] when they returned the next day it had filled in again.

I forgot to say the King's Head pub was on the roadside on its current site with a yard and stables at the back. I think the hunt used to meet there, but I am not sure. On the junction of Grimsby Road and Station Road was Brigg's Yard (livestock transporters) giving it the name of 'Briggies Corner'. Joe Atkinson's father had two fields (now Mill View) where he kept milkers.

Waltham had a very good brass band. They were mostly local chaps, including two of my brothers. I enjoyed attending their rehearsals in the loft at the back of Adams' shop and also in the Temperance Hall. I went with them to Belle Vue, Manchester where they took part in a band contest. At Christmas they went round the Village playing carols and certain big houses invited them inside to play – it was a lovely atmosphere. One Christmas I went on their rounds with a collecting box. It must have been in the early '50s because I was in army uniform and my National Service was '52-'54.

The carrier's horse-drawn cart run by Harold Rimmington was a regular part of life. He stood in the Bull Ring Grimsby with many other carriers.

Apologies for any errors but I am sure someone can correct them and I hope I have remembered most things correctly.

My ten years older brother has reminded me of more farms, e.g. Pepper's (opposite Boundary Rod) – hence Pepper's Hill – Ward's (next to Topliss shop) Hannington's (Gy Pea Bung fame) Cheapside. He also reminded me that Firs Farm, Cheapside belonged to Markhams before Wilkinson – different family to Markhams on Grove Lane side of Cheapside. The church also had two fields which they used to rent out, these were behind High Street where the Leas School and Dorothy and Danesfield Avenues now stand.

Jobs done in my schooldays include errand lad (Topliss), milk round (Markham) both on carrier bikes, potato picking, beet singling and topping, leading the horses between the stooks at harvest, tenting cows, i.e. keeping them off a certain crop in the field. I also used to drove Joe Atkinson's store cattle from Waltham to Tetney all for the princely sum of 1s – equalling 5p per hour. I was by no means unique in this as most of my school pals did the same, including the girls.

Allen Parker

❧ Three ❧

People and Characters

In a small community certain characters always stand out and are remembered by many people: the postmaster Horace Kendall, the village bobby Sgt Harbuttle, William Horn who lived at the rectory and wore a straw boater, Drs McKane and Chidlow, William Topliss the shopkeeper and his assistant Miss Patchett and not forgetting the 'Dillymen' who had the unenviable job of emptying the village earth closets! These people, and many others mentioned in this chapter, are long gone, but the descriptions given by the contributors have brought an added colour and dimension to the history of the village.

Coloured aspirins

Mr Woodforth was the saddler and the saddlery shop was in the High Street on the same side as Swags and Tails, not where our present-day saddlery is. The building which houses Swags and Tails used to be two houses. Jessie Woodforth, the saddler's daughter, lived in one of them and Mrs Hemmingfield would visit her and watch her eating grapes for breakfast. She married Percy Croft the coal man.

Kirks were 'gentlemen farmers' and although their farm is long gone, the avenue of trees near the Lodge on Barnoldby Road gives a sense of what was once there. One of the Kirk family also lived in Pear Tree cottage.

Jack Harrison and his family were the chicken farmers. He had brothers and sisters called Alf, Dan, Clarice, Jack and Sam. The farm was where the animal feed merchant's is now.

Evelyn Briggs. (Courtesy of Mrs E. Hemmingfield)

Dr McKane had an open car and a chauffeur. His dispensary was in the house which was situated at the end of Cheapside, near the Cenotaph, and he would dispense coloured aspirins for which you had to pay.

Evelyn Hemmingfield

Someone appeared from the house carrying a pair of old swords

Crossing over the road from Cheesemans Lane brings us into New Road. This road holds many memories, for it was here that I attended the Methodist school from an early age.

The cottages that stood at the junction of Skinners Lane and New Road were demolished when the corner was widened and replaced with modern bungalows. My old school chum David Stringer lived at No. 33, Edith Cook at 35 and Henry Leary at No. 37. Across the road, at No. 38, were the Stamford family. Ann Markham at No. 36, Miss Dora Sempers who was a close friend of my dad lived at No. 34, whilst Joseph Dunham lived at No. 32. Facing the school at No. 30 lived the Hutson family. This house has now been demolished, but was the former home of Captain Lewis who served in the Veterinary Corps during the First World War. His

New Road cottages, school house and barber's shop (date unknown). (North East Lincolnshire Council Libraries)

hobby was woodwork. I have some of his wooden planes stamped with his name. I well remember his chattels being auctioned following his death as I was standing in the school playground by the gates when someone appeared from the house carrying a pair of old swords.

I can still recall the names of some of the residents who lived in the cottages beyond the barber's shop: Nellie Maskel and Alwyn Markham, plus Iris Humphrey and Harry Tyas. 'Kirkdale', the villa on the corner of Cross Street, was the residence of Clive Browne and his family. Clive Browne was an art teacher, an MA and a member of the Royal Academy of Art. On the opposite corner stands the 'Hollies', the former home of Mr Topliss, grocer and draper.

Phil Young, a taxi proprietor and first postmaster of the new post office, lived in the bungalow next to the Hollies. During the war Phil was engaged on the construction of Waltham Airfield. Saxon House next to the church was the residence of Mr Thornton the sexton. The large building in the yard of the property was formerly the workshop of Wright & Sons, carpenters and wheelwrights.

Peter Burns

A mysterious lady

Barry remembers visiting Waltham many times in his youth. He remembers being told by his father about a concert at Welholme school that had been organised

WALTHAM, near GRIMSBY.

TO BE SOLD

By Auction

BY

MR. C. NAINBY,

ON THE PREMISES OF MR. RICHARD FAULDING, OF WALTHAM,
(Who is giving up his Farm,)

On THURSDAY, the 11th day of MAY, 1854,

The following Valuable Household

FURNITURE

NAMELY,—

Set of Mahogany Dining Tables, 8½ feet long, Mahogany Pembroke Table, Mahogany Round Tea Table, Mahogany Stand, Mahogany Desk, 9 Mahogany Chairs, Mahogany Night-Commode, Fine-toned Piano-Forte by Broadwood, Sofa in mahogany frame, hair stuffed, with rich chintz cover and cushions, Wainscot Stand and Cover, Globe Barometer, Wall Glass in gilt frame, Brass Fender and Fire-irons, Ash-Pan, Carpet 5 yards square, very little worse for wear, Mahogany Knife Tray, Sets of Mahogany Chamber Drawers, Painted and other Dressing Tables, do. Washstand and Towel Horses, several Sets of Chamber Chairs, Deal Wardrobe, 1 Four-post Bedstead with Chintz Furniture and Mattress, 1 Four-post Bedstead, 2 Camp Bedsteads and Furniture, 5 Mahogany Chairs, 2 Stump Bedsteads, 2 Feather Beds, Bolsters, and Mattress, 2 Large Kitchen Tables with drawers, 1 Round do., Flour Bin with three partitions, 4 Wood-bottomed Chairs, Large Fender and Fire-irons, Culinary and Earthenware, Dairy and Brewing Utensils, with sundry other Articles too tedious for the limits of a hand-bill.

**At the same time will be Sold
7 SIDES OF BACON, with the HAMS,**

THE SALE TO COMMENCE AT HALF-PAST TWELVE O'CLOCK

SKELTON PRINTER, MARKET-PLACE, GRIMSBY.

A notice for a furniture auction, 1854. (Skelton Collection, North East Lincolnshire Council Libraries)

to raise money for Belgian refugees. The money raised was presented to Lady Eugenia Doughty of Waltham.

Villagers included Charlie Mountain at the old King's Head, Minnie Markham, who lived on the corner of Elm Road, and a mysterious lady who used to swirl around the village in a long cloak. There was also Mrs Oole, who lived in a white cottage on Barnoldby Road, Len Stephenson and Phil Young, who were the postmasters and Sid Farr, who had land near the garage on Brigsley Road.

Kirks' Farm was along Barnoldby Road and was a lovely old farmhouse owned by the Kirk family who came from Thorganby.

Barry Herbert

I remember going with my father to collect the rents

My father, Clarence Charles White, was born in 1901 at Cheapside in a house owned by his parents and [it was] left to my father at their deaths, together with the shop and cottages. As a young boy I remember going with my father to collect the rents – I seem to think 2s 6d the small cottages, 7s 6d the larger and 15s Cheapside house.

My grandparents retired to a newish bungalow just off the Barnoldby Road next door to a young Eric Burton (Burton's Garage, Wellowgate). I think the Cheapside House tenant was a Mr Raymond and the blacksmith's house was

Waltham veterans, c. 1947. From left to right: George Davey (or Tharratt?), Ted Ladlow, William Hickson, Joe Craggs. (North East Lincolnshire Council Libraries)

Census for 1901 showing George White, blacksmith, and his wife Martha. (Courtesy of Proquest)

sold to a sea captain. The small cottages were sold in 1938/39 for £100 each and Cheapside I think for £750. My father gave the shop to Harry Jackson as he had never been charged for rent.

The neighbours to Cheapside House were the Hewitts [Victoria Street] – jewellers – there was a paddock between where my grandfather kept his pony which my father used to ride to school. The last owner of the Hewitts' house I knew was Frank Waddingham, the dentist.

My father went to St James's School, Grimsby. A friend of his was Clive Browne, schoolmaster and talented artist. I have one of his windmill pictures dated 1973 [Waltham Mill]. He, as you probably know, lived at Waltham.

David White

The Dillymen

For the people of Waltham the Dillymen were regular visitors. There were two Dilly men – Ben Aisthorpe and Ben Grimoldby. Once one of them dropped his sandwiches into the dilly cart, which was full of the waste they had emptied from the earth closets. Did he eat them? You bet! He decided they would be fine as they were wrapped in greaseproof paper!

Cynthia Appleton, Derrick Coop and Christine Tindall

The blacksmith's house and smithy, 1943. (North East Lincolnshire Council Libraries)

Cheapside and smithy, 1968. (North East Lincolnshire Council Libraries)

Now then mate, we'd better 'ave a settle up!

'Cozzie Johnson' was the man who cleaned out the drains in the village and he was known as the 'lengthsman'. He would clear Buck Beck, which runs through the village and wore waders for his work. When he went to the pub after work he would turn his waders down.

Charlie Mountain's sister, Lily, ran the King's Head. Charlie was a real character, a wonderful character. He was a keen cyclist and was also known for having a good memory for dates – especially which horse won the Derby and when! When the 'new' King's Head was built Florence Mountain, Lily's daughter, who married Bob Watkinson, became the landlady and Bob, the landlord. Lily's other daughter Mary married Ted Pick the dentist.

Horace Kendall was the bell ringer and postmaster of Waltham in the days before the Second World War. If you wanted to make a phone call in the night, Horace would have to be woken up to connect you – and would be none too pleased about it! This work of course pre-dated the telephone exchange, which came to the village in later years.

Charles Brears was the first head of Waltham Toll Bar School. He was the author of the *History of Waltham* in the 1930s. I was at school with his son, Reginald, at Clee Grammar.

King's Head with Nell and Florence Mountain, c. 1901. (Courtesy of Mrs E. Hemmingfield)

Old man Harrison would allow farmers to have a year's credit then at harvest time he would say 'Now then mate, we'd better 'ave a settle up!'. He was a very astute business man – it was a form of bartering which resulted in self-sufficiency and co-operation amongst the villagers.

Sid Farr was reputed to be a real cowboy! He taught people how to ride and wore a stetsun – he had even travelled to America. He owned the land which runs from Norman Corner to the next corner where the new housing development known as Brigsley Grange has been built.

Harriet Lawrence has been described as a mysterious witch-like woman who swirled around the village in long robes. She lived at No. 21 Kirkgate. Nowadays she would simply be described as eccentric, but if children bothered her by banging on her door she would appear brandishing a carving knife!

Bill Adams

She knitted in the corner whilst waiting for patients

People remember Sergeant Harbuttle, the village policeman, who knew everyone. Mr Parker of Church Lane used to keep pigs behind Topliss shop. He could be seen staggering across the road carrying buckets of pigswill. Mr Harland was a qualified gardener and was deaf as a post. He loved classical music and it could regularly be heard blaring out of his cottage. His son was a milkman and window cleaner. Old Mrs Pepper of Pepper's Hill held a surgery once a week in her back room. There was newspaper on the floor in the front room which served as a waiting room. She knitted in the corner whilst waiting for patients. Dr Asche, a Polish Jew, was a doctor in the village. He was about eighty-three when he left and was succeeded by Dr Hicks in the High Street. One lady recalled that all his medical records were rolled up together and secured with rubber bands. He used to boil up needles and syringes.

There were eight boys in the Parker family and one girl. All the boys had nicknames.

Harriet Lawrence lived in Kirkgate. She wore long black crinolins and a veil. When she died she was carried from Trail Poke Lane and buried in the church.

The Dillymen would come along with their wooden cart to empty the earth closets of waste. The waste was spread onto the meadows in Ings Lane. The Dillymen would 'skell' the waste. ['Skelling' is an old Lincolnshire word which was defined by Edward Campinon in his *Lincolnshire Dialects*: 'The old fashioned horse-drawn farm cart was constructed so that it could be tipped to discharge or skell a load by withdrawing a pin that secured the body to the shafts.']

Reminiscence session, Waltham Library, 21 November 2008

❧ Four ❧

Streets and Houses

Many of the streets and houses described in this chapter still exist today, but their surroundings have changed beyond recognition.

During the latter part of the twentieth century Waltham grew from a population of just over 2,000 in 1951 to over 6,000 inhabitants in 2001 (figures from the Office for National Statistics ONS). This is reflected in the huge housing developments along Barnoldby Road and stretching into Bradley Road and Brigsley Road. Many people now live in Waltham but work elsewhere.

Mid-twentieth-century Waltham is remembered as an essentially rural village with agriculture and farming at the heart of its existence. There are fond memories of walking along Barnoldby Road when it was no more than fields and happy days spent 'wooding' and collecting brambles or picking potatoes.

If you needed your chickens despatching he was the man to call

I was born in Waltham in 1946 and over the years I have seen many changes. My earliest recollections date from around 1950 as I spent most of my first four years being looked after by my grandparents, who lived in Waltham Road Scartho, just beyond the boundary with the village.

Markham's Farm on Waltham Road was known then as Pepper's Farm, and a footpath on that side of the road continued to the junction of Toll Bar/High Street corner. Travelling along the Grimsby Road on the right-hand side towards the village, just past the first few houses, there stood an ancient ash tree and in the

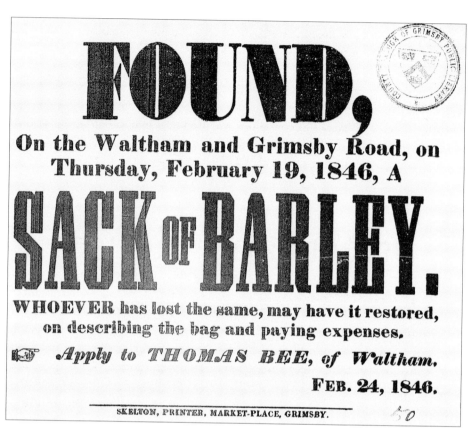

FOUND,

On the Waltham and Grimsby Road, on Thursday, February 19, 1846, A

SACK OF BARLEY.

WHOEVER has lost the same, may have it restored, on describing the bag and paying expenses.

☞ *Apply to THOMAS BEE, of Waltham.*

FEB. 24, 1846.

SKELTON, PRINTER, MARKET-PLACE, GRIMSBY.

Notice for sack of barley found on the Waltham and Grimsby Road, 1846. (Skelton Collection, North East Lincolnshire Council Libraries)

adjacent field local football teams had a pitch and played matches on Saturdays. Just beyond this point there were the remains of a Blast Shelter left over from the war. This was erected for the use of bus passengers caught in an air raid.

Then came the brow of Pepper's Hill where Mr Moggridge had a small holding and kept geese. If you needed your chickens despatching he was the man to call. During the winter months, when in those days we used to get a lot of snow, Pepper's Hill became impassable for there were not many cars about then – if you spotted four a day you were lucky.

Proceeding along Grimsby Road the building on the left-hand side (which is now a vet's) was built during the war and used as a hostel for the Land Army girls and later on became the first Leas school. During the war a barricade was put across the road by the Home Guard. According to neighbours, they were armed with one rifle and five rounds of ammunition between six of them.

The houses along Grimsby Road at this period of time were mostly owned by fish merchants and retired business people. It was known then as 'Nobs Row' and was quite an affluent area. The junction of Grimsby Road and the High Street was known as Briggs Corner after Harry Briggs, whose farm was located there. I knew the farmer's son and had to remember to don my wellies when visiting him for you were up to your ankles in cow muck. We used to watch them threshing corn, the old machine being driven by a grey Ferguson tractor – happy days! Across the road stood the original telephone exchange, now converted into a bungalow.

Peter Burns

You could go and get the milk in a can with a lid on it

From when I was seven, we moved to just round this corner here and my friend lived on that corner of Cheesemans Lane. It's named after a councillor I believe from the '20s or perhaps even before. And it was just a lane; at the bottom of the lane was a stile, or about half way down, and you went across another field to the farm for the milk, because even when I was little you could go and get the milk in a can with a lid on it. We used to go over the stile and across to the farm to get the milk of a morning. I don't know whether that farm's still there. There were two and they belonged to brothers.

Ivy cottage, I think a relation of my mother's lived there and I think in later years she had a new bungalow built around the corner and lived there until she went into a home. Just around the corner was a thatched cottage, I don't know whether that's still there. But it's all houses there now.

I don't remember the thatched cottage in Church Lane. It wasn't thatched when I was young, but the farm was there; I used to go and play there. We knew everybody that lived along there. A couple lived on the end, and their son went to be a missionary in Montego Bay; he was killed there. We were at school together. The couple were called Mr and Mrs Pegg. Steven Pegg was the name of the son and he was the same age as me, and when he was in his twenties he went to theological college and when he was finished he went as a missionary to Montego Bay; he went all around there but that is were he finished. He'd got a car. He wasn't the kind of person that you would think would be a missionary. He was always full of fun and first in trouble, we used to get into quite a bit of trouble and it was always his fault.

The family that lived in the next house, there was a lot of children – I should think about nine, maybe more. The mother used to be a maid at the mill for a little while, when she was about thirteen or fourteen. My mother always called her Lizzy, but I think it was probably Elizabeth Sheffings and her married name was

Parker. One of the sons lived next door to my mum and dad when they retired and lived in a bungalow up Manor Drive. They are still alive, the couple. The lady [Mrs Parker] I think she recently died; she was something like 108 or 109. She had a hard life because there were at least nine children, maybe more. They were always happy and she always seemed a happy kind of a lady, but of course I was little as well, you don't take that much notice. I don't remember her husband; I don't know if he had died maybe when I was younger.

Barbara West

Adventurous boys in those carefree days

At the beginning of the High Street on the left-hand side stood the remains of the officers' quarters for the wartime airbase, RAF Grimsby. These were occupied by Grimsby people who had been bombed out during the war and they were known as the squatters' huts. Legend has it that a certain woman from Grimsby asked the local bobby if she and her family could move into the empty accommodation. His reply was that she could do what she liked as it was nothing to do with him! Word spread on the bush telegraph and the place was overrun with squatters. The Borough Council had no option but to renovate the huts and install electricity and proper sanitation, for the residents were cooking on open fires and using oil lamps for illumination. These huts remained occupied until the Grimes Green Estate, now known as Fairway, was built. They remained derelict for several years, becoming an ideal playground for us adventurous boys in those carefree days.

Across the road, where the entrance to Danesfield Avenue is now located, was a field in which Mr Marsh the one-armed man kept the horse to pull his cart and by the gateway stood a conker tree. You had to watch out when collecting conkers for his horse was a stallion and could give you a nasty bite. Next to this field entrance is located the home of the Lock family. Mr Lock used to have a horse-drawn fairground caravan in his garden, which he used for a workshop in conjunction with his amusement business.

Further down the High Street you come to a large house with a green roof. This was the doctor's residence and surgery. The first doctor I can recall was Dr Chidlow who used to keep a pair of bullmastiff dogs and one day as I was leaving school they had somehow got out and as I passed the gateway of the doctor's, they pounced on me pinning me to the ground and they had to be pulled off me by a passer-by. Fortunately, I was only shaken up a bit. I was about six years old at the time but still remember the incident well after all these years. When Dr Chidlow retired, the practice was taken over by Dr Fisher, a canny Scotsman who did not suffer fools gladly. However, he was an excellent doctor. The High

Waltham rectory in the 1950s.
(North East Lincolnshire
Council Libraries)

Street beyond the doctor's residence has seen many changes over the years and much redevelopment has taken place.

Manor Drive was then a lane, the only development being the Smedleys' Fishermen's Cottages, the lane then leading to a block of houses surrounded by open fields.

The road passing the church beyond Manor Drive was very narrow and winding, large trees overhung the road from the churchyard and a high brick wall surrounded the remains of the Old Hall which was in a poor state of repair and owned by the Hoole family. During the war the Old Hall was used as the officers' mess for RAF Grimsby. Visibility was very poor on this stretch of road and though there was not much motor traffic, I became a casualty. The year was 1956 and I was crossing the road from Church Lane after leaving school. I was struck down by a motor scooter, suffering a fractured skull and a broken jaw. Dr Fisher was called to the scene and rumour spread that he had knocked me down with his car – the perils of the bush telegraph.

I remember coming round briefly in the gardener's cottage at the Old Hall where Nurse Mackrill, the local district nurse and midwife, resided before I was rushed off to the old General Hospital. After this event a school crossing sign was erected. It was one of the old cast-iron type and it remained until the flashing crossing lights were installed. At least some good came of my misfortune.

After passing the church and coming to the top of Ludgate Hill, adjacent to the cake shop and beyond where the library now stands was the original Old Rectory, Revd Geipel being the vicar.

Peter Burns

A lot of the older folk still call it Doctors' Corner

The blacksmith's was on Cheapside until I was about ten or twelve; he kept going mending gates and bikes and things, he did shoe some horses when we were younger. They call the corner of Cheapside 'Doctors' Corner', because on the corner was a big house and a doctor lived in it, and they always called it Doctors' Corner and a lot of the older folk still call it Doctors' Corner. The younger ones won't know half of what people are talking about these days because a lot of the streets have different names to what people call them and my mother always called them by their old names. I can't remember a doctor living there since well into the '60s so it's forty-odd years, probably, since a doctor actually lived there. I bet there are still people that live in the village that call it Doctors' Corner. On the other corner now it's the Cenotaph. I think they put that up after the Second World War, but I'm not sure, it could have been the First. They had it somewhere else, I think, after the First World War, and then they put it on the corner, but it's been moved a time or two. Not very much, but back a bit because they widened the road.

Every Remembrance Sunday we went to the Cenotaph, I think they still do. Everybody in the village went in those days when we were younger because nearly everybody had known somebody in one of the wars, and our parents had taken part one way or another. So it was instilled into you, but it was nice because it was everybody together and you knew everybody, which is sad now because you don't. I think the last time I went … I didn't see a single person I knew. Before I got married, if I'd have walked down the High Street, I wouldn't have gone half a dozen paces before I met someone I knew.

Cheapside and Cenotaph in the 1920s (above) and 2005 (below). There has been much discussion over the years as to whether the Cenotaph was moved, but these photographs demonstrate that the Cenotaph was not moved but the direction of the road was altered. (North East Lincolnshire Council Libraries)

The bus always came right round this corner [corner of Cheapside], and if you lived down the other way they would jump off at the corner. The conductor used to stand there shouting 'nobody jump', and they did as soon as it slowed to go round the corner, everybody jumped off. There were seats at the back of Cheapside. We used to sit there a lot, congregate, when we were younger because there weren't that many places to go, but everybody used to go on Armistice Sunday, lay wreaths and the British Legion in the village went, all the old soldiers. It was a much more gentle time really. I don't know anybody that's on the memorial; fortunately, we never lost anyone during either war, that I know of anyway.

Barbara West

Waltham shooting affray

The Waltham shooting affray took place on 31 March 1910 and was reported with the headline 'Alleged Attempted Murder' in the local newspaper of that time. At about 6.20 p.m. on 31 March 1910 two cyclists stopped at the Waltham Toll House, an isolated spot in those days on the road from Waltham to the railway station at what is now New Waltham.

Toll Bar Cottage, 1924. (North East Lincolnshire Council Libraries)

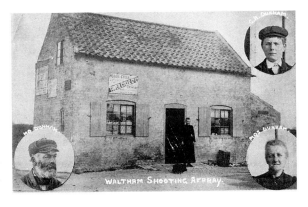

The house was owned by a Mr and Mrs Dunham and they ran a 'pop shop' providing refreshments for travellers and passers-by. The two cyclists were John Gosling and his friend Herbert Charles Russell. The cyclists spent some time chatting in the shop then suddenly, without warning, pulled a gun and demanded money. Mrs Dunham was shot in the neck and Mr Dunham gave chase to the robbers. The police and Dr McKane arrived almost at the same time and luckily Mrs Dunham survived.

Descriptions of the two men were given to the police and after only three days the two men were arrested. Their trial took place on 5 April 1910 in the Brighowgate Courthouse in Grimsby and witnesses included Mr Charles Mountain, son of the licensee of the King's Head, Waltham.

Gosling was found guilty of unlawful wounding and sentenced to four months' hard labour. Russell was discharged with a warning.

[A full write-up of this event was published in the *Grimsby Telegraph Bygones* on 8 and 9 July 2008. You can also read the original report in the *Grimsby Telegraph* 31 March 1910 which is kept on microfilm in Grimsby Reference and Local History Library, North East Lincolnshire.]

There was a robbery there

I don't remember the toll house being there, I don't know if it was there in my day, this was on the other side to where Toll Bar School is and you used to have to pay a toll to go on that road. I don't know which road the toll was for; I don't know if it was the one to Waltham or the one to Grimsby, or the one to Louth. The only thing I really know about that is that there was a robbery there. Two scoundrels from Grimsby had gone in and were going to beat them up. I think they tied up the man, because it was a couple, it was their home, and the woman saw them off with a broom or something. The robbers lived somewhere in Grimsby and the police knew where to find them. It's only hearsay that my mother had told me and my brother.

Barbara West

Waithe Road, Cheapside (date unknown). (North East Lincolnshire Council Libraries)

Waltham rectory in the 1950s. (North East Lincolnshire Council Libraries)

She was a woman who liked her ale

Trail Poke Lane became known as Fairway just before the Second World War. It possibly got that name because a 'poke' was a sack and people would trail the sacks behind them. Burma Road was at the back of Ings Lane and was a track which lead to the sewerage farm made during the Second World War. The bluestone, which is now on the village green, was originally on the corner of Cheapside and Kirkgate and was used as a mounting block. It can be seen on the photograph of the Church School. Mr Markham, a local farmer who was quite short and rotund, would tether his pony in the pub yard and on leaving the pub would have to lead his pony to the mounting block on Cheapside in order to be able to get on the pony.

Wright & Sons Wheelwright was down Cheapside. A fine example of how all trades were inter-dependent is the working relationship between the blacksmiths on Cheapside and the wheelwrights. There was a furnace behind the blacksmiths buildings on Cheapside. The wheelwrights would make the wheel and Harry Jackson the blacksmith would make the iron band to go round the wheel. The wheel was rolled along up the road to the blacksmiths where the iron band would be heated up in the furnace. When the iron band was hot the wheel would be anchored to the road through the axle hole and the band would be dropped onto the wheel. Water was then poured over the wheel to cool and shrink the iron band around it.

The oldest cottage is in Cheesemans Lane. It was originally called Rose Cottage but is now the Brambles. It was originally a 'wattle and daub' and thatched building.

The Tilted Barrel used to be a house owned by Byron Hickson. When the Tilted Barrel was just a house, it was owned by Byron Hickson's parents. Byron used to pump the organ at the church. Next to the Tilted Barrel were stable-type buildings which were owned by a cobbler with a Scandinavian name.

Kirkside cottages were only built in the 1930s. Before that, the land there backed onto the Manor House which stands next to Albion House on Cheapside.

The site now occupied by the library used to be a row of cottages which fronted straight onto the High Street. Aunt Ada Parlett lived in one of the cottages. She was a woman who liked her ale and would put on her shawl, take a jug to the King's Head and get it filled with ale, then make her way back home with the jug of ale under her shawl.

The builder who built many of the houses in Laburnum Avenue was called 'Sparrow Allison' – a stout fellow. The names of some of the families that lived there are Birkitt, Thornton, Amos, Lattimer, Smith, Buddy Rose, Granny Dobbs, Mr Shelley the organist, the Traffords and the Gutteridges.

Joe Atkinson was the farmer who owned the land where Mill View is now built. Cattle used to roam on the fields there.

Penny Mews was the first school in the village and the new flats there have retained the name. Children attending the school had to pay a penny. Waltham Old Hall was opposite the church. Waltham rectory was on the land which is now the village green; it was built in 1836. There is rumoured to be an inter-connecting network of tunnels which ran between Waltham Old Hall, the church and the rectory, although this has never been substantiated.

Bill Adams

A popular venue for dances

Taking a walk towards Barnoldby after leaving the shop once owned by Mr Topliss, and passing the quaint cottages preceding the Mews, we come to Rose Cottage, once owned by the Church Commissioners. After Rose Cottage the interesting old premises is that of Harrison's Corn and Seed Merchants. Formerly owned by Jack Harrison it was here that I used to go with my dad to purchase the feed for our chickens. Now I believe it is owned by his daughter, Lynn, with whom I attended school.

Further down the road is Pear Tree Cottage. This was once a farm before the building of the housing estate. Next is the Lodge, which formerly belonged to Barnoldby House, now surrounded by other dwellings, the house once stood by itself surrounded by fields. Opposite the junction of Barnoldby Road and Bradley Road is the brick yard pond, home of the 55 Angling Club, so named after the number of members, which was limited to 55. There was always a long waiting list of prospective members as one had to wait until a member died for a vacancy to occur. The brick yard was once owned by the Cheeseman family and produced many of the bricks used in the construction of Waltham properties. A pair of cottages once stood in the yard and these were at one period the home of the Cheffings family. My old school friend Norman Robertson lived in one of the cottages before they were demolished due to rising damp caused by the pond overflowing during heavy rain storms.

On the return journey to the village we come to the Ross Hall, the home of the British Legion Club and Institute. This was always a popular venue for dances and was much used by the airmen stationed at Waltham during the war. By all accounts many a liaison blossomed here. It was still a popular venue for entertainment during the 1970s and '80s when the late Jeff Griggs held sway.

At the junction of Barnoldby Road with the High Street, a right turn takes one into Brigsley Road. The second house on the right-hand side was, before its conversion to a private residence, the police house and station. During my childhood it was manned by Sergeant Harbottle and four constables. You had to

The High Street with the King's Head on left, 1950s. (North East Lincolnshire Council Libraries)

The High Street from Fairway corner, 1930s. (North East Lincolnshire Council Libraries)

keep a good look out when scrumping because, if you were caught, you received a clip round the ear before being taken home for another wallop from your dad. It never did us any harm and taught us boys to have respect for others.

In later years during the 1990s I served from here as a Special Constable alongside PC Bob Clarke. But that's another story ...

On the opposite side of the road much new building has taken place. Back in the late 1950s only two bungalows and five houses existed before the windmill site. Following the bungalows stood Hill Top Garage and service station. This garage dispensed BP petrol and it was here that my dad used to have his car serviced. Two semi-detached houses have now been built on its site. I will just give a mention to the vet Peter Hurst who had his veterinary practice at Waltham House, the former home during the nineteenth century of Major Thomas Coats.

Peter Burns

Just Acetylene lamps and candles

We lived in the cottage which is now occupied by Shires Restaurant in the High Street. It was known as Beverlac Cottage and had no electricity, just Acetylene lamps and candles. There was a larder where we would keep half a pig and the cottage also had a cellar.

Briggs Corner is named after the Briggs family who farmed there. Later, Harry Briggs had the cottage next to the fire station which is still there today. He had the haulage business. My grandfather came from Wyham near Louth. He was called John Peter Coulbeck Briggs and came to Waltham to work for Sir George Doughty. He was coachman to Sir George and used to take him up to the station at New Waltham to get the London train which would make a special stop for Sir George Doughty MP. After Sir George Doughty died, a lady called Nurse Mackrill lived at Waltham Old Hall with her sister, but they only occupied two of the many rooms.

The Hollies was occupied by the Hewitt family and I can remember being given 1d a week for taking Arthur Hewitt to school.

Waltham Tea Gardens was also used as the tennis centre and people would arrive in waggonettes. It belonged to White's, who had two daughters – May and Edie.

Salisbury Drive was Glebe land owned by the church. It was used for allotments before the current houses were built there in the early 1950s.

There were no houses where the Cenotaph is now – just open fields between Kirkgate and the High Street and the circus would visit and use this site.

Evelyn Hemmingfield

Brigg Corner in the 1930s. (North East Lincolnshire Council Libraries)

Church Lane

Taking a short cut through the churchyard and passing on the right-hand side, the grave of Sir George Doughty JP MP of Waltham Old Hall, who died on the 27 April 1914, brings one onto Church Lane. The semi derelict cottage next to the churchyard was formerly the home of Mrs Ballans, owner of the former wool shop. The row of cottages adjacent have, in the course of time, received several make-overs and no longer resemble the simple lines of agricultural workers' abodes remembered from my childhood.

Now renamed The Stables, the former coach house on the corner of Cross Street, which used to belong to the Topliss family, has been saved and converted into residential use. I passed this building many times *en route* to and from the school in New Road. The listing of the building towards the pavement becoming more evident as the years passed. It was used in my school days to house the car owned by Sidney Topliss. Unfortunately, I cannot remember the make of the vehicle, which was even then something of a classic. Sadly, Mr Topliss died at the

Kirkgate, c. 1910. (North East Lincolnshire Council Libraries)

wheel of this car, which overturned, crushing its roof. However, his lady passenger escaped serious injury. When the damaged vehicle was sold after languishing in the yard of Pete Spence the motor engineer, the new owner simply bashed out the crushed roof with a sledge hammer!

On the corner of Cross Street, the coach house and stable at the rear of Kirkdale, the former home of Clive Browne, remain unaltered. During the 1980s the hayloft was used to store the camping equipment belonging to the 2nd Waltham Scout Group. On the corner of the lane leading to Ashlea Court Residential Home, which was built on the site of Portas [*sic*] & Son's engineering works, stands an old detached house with possible late Georgian origins. Adjacent to this house, now completely revamped, stands the property formerly named Cross Ways – its origins possibly connected to farming. During my school days it was the residence of Charles Harrison. Connected to the main building was a low-roofed structure formerly used as a dairy.

Facing No. 7 is Worsley House, the former home of Fred and Rose Buffam. The cottages standing beyond this point have also received make-overs during the past decade. Number 24 was the former residence of John Wilkinson, whilst at No. 26 lived Bert Wilson. This property has been named the Coach House owing to the building at the rear of the premises being formerly used as a stable and coach house. This building backs onto the playground of the Methodist School.

Jack Cowley lived at No. 28, whilst at No. 30 lived William Field and at No. 32 Frank Parker. John Pegg lived at No. 34 and the unforgettable Bessie Tharatt occupied the house at the end of the road. On the opposite side of Church Lane, just prior to its junction with Skinners Lane, stands No. 31, Church Farm, once the residence of George Archer. The farmyard has been completely redeveloped in recent times; however, back in my school days it was a working dairy farm. Prior to Church Farm, at No. 27 lived my school friend Billy Strugnell. Billy and his brother Bobby were well known for riding Velocette motorcycles around the locality. Billy was a good friend who stood up for me against the school bullies. He still drives around the village but the days of motorcycling are long gone.

Peter Burns

She used to knit for the troops all through the war

My friend's mother lived down Front Street (now High Street); a big family, there was about seven of them, and my mother used to go to tea sometimes on a Sunday. We used to stand up to eat because there was so many of them, they all stood around the table, and after tea they would all go off to play. I don't know why they called it Front Street, but it was always Front Street to us and Ludgate Hill.

There was a wool shop or haberdashery shop, and one or two houses down was the pub – it came straight onto the pavement then, so anybody that got chucked out, they landed on the pavement outside. Before that, or just after, was the post office, and it was what looked like a front room. One of the people that lived there – her name was Lancaster and, as far as I know, she was never married – was in a wheel chair. I don't know whether she had had polio or something when she was young. She used to knit for the troops all through the war evidently. Some time ago she got some kind of recognition or something because there is a memorial up along the road. She died recently, but she used to sit outside in her wheelchair. I don't know if it was her brother who was the postman, and he knew every single person in the village and what post you'd had, he could tell your neighbour what post you'd had, and you what they had got.

The church hall was there; it was there when I was younger anyway because all the village functions were held there, my mothers silver wedding anniversary, and loads of wedding receptions and things. There was a lovely double-fronted haberdashery shop at the top of the hill, there was some really nice buildings

Cheapside and the Methodist Church, c. 1924. (North East Lincolnshire Council Libraries)

Waltham Cenotaph, 2005. (North East Lincolnshire Council Libraries)

looking back now, but of course in the sixties they went mad pulling everything down and modernising, which is a shame really.

Trail Poke Lane, that's Fairway. I have no idea why they called it that but maybe it's because they took the pigs up there that way, because there was a pig farm around there. There was fields all behind there and we used to go and play, Mount Pleasant it is now. There was a cricket pitch, a football pitch; I think it's similar now. They had loads of teams in the village playing cricket and what have you, because all the villages and Grimsby had teams and they all used to play each other. There wasn't a lot of other things to do. They used to play cricket up there a lot, but of course being a girl, and in those days, you didn't play much of those sorts of things. I never went up there very much, but my brothers did.

Barbara West

A spooky experience

Just beyond the Cenotaph stood the blacksmith's shop on Cheapside which was bounded on either side by a pair of cottages. It was here that I spent many a time watching Harry Jackson, the blacksmith, working at the forge and occasionally shoeing horses. I always wanted to be a blacksmith and asked Harry if he would take me on as his apprentice – sadly Harry said he was too old and times were changing with new regulations in force. Had he been younger he would have been pleased to take me on.

I had to settle on joinery, though I did learn to work a forge at night school and produced some interesting pieces of work. The skills I learnt enabled me to make the rudder fittings for the shrimper *Perseverance*, which is preserved at the Fishing Heritage Centre.

Across the road from the smithy stands the Hollies, where lived Frank Waddingham. Thomas Chambers lived at the Manor House, whilst Albion House was the home of Dennis Marsh. Albion House had a small ship's bell mounted above the door. Was this, I wonder, a relic of HMS *Albion*? Also above the door frame was the carved head of a lion which was painted red, perhaps its origin will now also be revealed.

The Temperance Hall was where the founding meeting of the Windmill Preservation Society was held. Just beyond this building stood the Methodist hall. Although I cannot remember attending any events held at this place I remember the building itself.

Crossing back over the road is the Methodist chapel where, for a short while, I attended Sunday school, later married and where my son was christened by the Revd Robinson. The cottage at the end of the row beyond the chapel was the home of Raymond Wilson, the plumber. This brings us to the junction with Skinners Lane. Facing the lane in the 1950s a derelict shed stood there covering a pair of steam ploughing engines. I guess they were cut up for scrap as they had disappeared by 1960. Just beyond this shed was the entrance to the former RAF Medical Quarters; the barrier across the entrance still had its fire bell *in situ*. This bell, I believe, was later mounted on the wall of Tan Yard Cottage, but disappeared sometime before the Tan Yard site was redeveloped.

Continuing along Cheapside we come to the White House, once the home of Mr and Mrs Jack. Some of the flower containers in the garden were constructed from bomb casings left over from the wartime airbase and remained *in situ* for many years. Passing the infill of new bungalows stand three cottages. The end cottage, now extended, was originally during the 1900s the home of the wheelwright/joiner and undertaker, John Allison. The forge that stood in the yard has recently been demolished and the tyre bending rollers that stood outside appear to have gone for scrap.

The large house that stands on the corner with Elm Road was once the residence of my uncle, the late Wink Pearson, who stood as unsuccessful Conservative candidate for Grimsby at the General Elections of 1954 and 1959. Beyond this point stands Elms Dyke Cottage, the home then of Ernest Dawson. After this comes Poplar Farm, then the abode of John Harrison. At the entrance to the airfield was the guard house, complete with cells; this was used as a joiner's shop by Pete Plant, who lived at Brigsley. Returning along Cheapside and venturing a short distance down Grove lane, we come to Landore, a late Victorian villa. Facing this property once stood the kitchens for the wartime airbase. These remained in a derelict state for many years before being demolished to make way for the residence of John Snape the builder.

Just before this point is the snicket that cuts through into Cheesemans Lane. Much redevelopment has taken place in this lane, several cottages have gone and new bungalows have replaced them. Two detached villas, including Winterwood, remain, as does Cheesemans House, once the residence of the brickyard owner during the 1950s – Frederick Tatman lived here. It was at this house that I had a spooky experience. During the late 1960s I was engaged by new owners to lay a new wooden floor in the lounge. These premises were unoccupied and before going for my lunch break I left my joiner's square at the entrance door to the lounge, there being no floor boards, only joists. On my return I discovered my square had been moved across the other side of the room. During my time working at the house I always felt a presence in the room although I was the only person there.

Over the road from Cheesemans House once stood White Gates Cottage, the oldest cottage in the village, built of mud and stud construction and originally thatched. It was sadly demolished, despite attempts to have a preservation order placed on it. Where No. 1 Cheesemans Lane now stands there was a wooden bungalow owned by the late Mrs Smith of Skinners Lane. Only the outside box toilet remains in the garden of the replacement bungalow.

Peter Burns

You all put your best clothes on and off you went

Heather Brackenbury lived with her mum and dad in a house that's the Tilted Barrel now. Her mother's maiden name was Coop. They came back to the village when Heather was thirteen, in about 1960. Her mother, after she left school, went into service. Up Brigsley Road there is a house, and it was the Robinsons that lived there and I think it was a small holding. They'd no family or anything and Heather's mother used to be their maid, or housekeeper. She worked for them until she got married. When they got married they went to live near Lincoln because

The Cabin. (By Katie Wilson, Leas Junior School)

WALTHAM,

IN THE BOROUGH OF GRIMSBY.

ELIGIBLE FREEHOLD BUILDING LAND.

To be Sold by Auction,

BY MR. CHARLES NAINBY,

AT THE KING'S HEAD INN, IN WALTHAM,

ON THURSDAY, THE 21ST DAY OF SEPTEMBER, NEXT,

At the hour of FOUR in the Afternoon; (subject to such Conditions as shall be then produced;)

THE FOLLOWING VERY VALUABLE

FREEHOLD ESTATE,

SITUATE AT WALTHAM, IN THE COUNTY OF LINCOLN;

COMPRISING

A Farm House, Stable and Outbuildings, Yards, Gardens, and Paddock thereto belonging; a Messuage, Grocer's Shop, and Garden, and about Six Acres of Land, eligibly situate for Building Purposes, near to the Church, and at the entrance to the Village of Waltham, and containing altogether

10A. 1R. 22P.,

Which will be offered in the following or such other Lots as may be agreed upon at the time of Sale, namely :—

LOT 1.—All that Brick and Tiled MESSUAGE and GROCER'S SHOP, in the occupation of John Bond, together with the Garden Ground behind the same, containing in the whole...**718 square yards.**

LOT 2.—All that PLOT of GARDEN GROUND, adjoining Lot 1 on the North East, having frontages of 52 feet on the North West to the Town Street, of an average depth of 168 feet 9 inches, and containing .... **1002 square yards.**

LOT 3.—All that other PLOT of GARDEN GROUND, adjoining Lot 2 on the North East, having a frontage of 52 feet to the said Town Street, and of an average depth of 172 feet 9 inches, containing .... **1009 square yards.**

LOT 4.—All that PLOT of GRASS LAND, (being part of a Close on the South side of the Church, lately occupied by Richard Faulding), behind Lots 1, 2 and 3, and having a frontage of 272 feet on the East to an intended new road of the width of 30 feet, leading from the Church, bounded on the West by Buck Beck, and South by Lot 5, and containing................................**5391 square yards.**

Sale of land in Waltham leaflet, 1854. (Courtesy of L. Norris)

he (Charles Brackenbury) was a farm labourer … so they went out there to live. Farm work got less and less and then her husband worked for a building firm and they moved back here to the Tilted Barrel. They moved back about 1960 and they lived there until a good while after Heather got married. The Tilted Barrel is supposed to be haunted as well. You could hear footsteps upstairs. I stayed several times and you could hear footsteps. I don't know how old the house actually is. It is a big house and she (Heather) said to me about these foot steps several times; they often heard these footsteps walking about.

There was a shop on the corner belonging to Harrison's, which is the cake shop now. Harrison's, they got a corn merchants down Barnoldby Road. The big field, they used to always have the Whit Weekend Gala on Whit Monday and you all put your best clothes on and off you went. They had a fancy-dress competition – which was what my mother won several times, once dressed as a set of traffic lights in 1927 when she was sixteen – and pin the tail on the donkey, all sorts of games and things and across the road was the British Legion.

Barbara West

There was no running water

In 1953 Mrs Tindall and her husband moved into a railway carriage which was situated in Laburnum Avenue and had previously been occupied by a family called Desforges. There was no running water inside the carriage, just a cold water tap outside. No toilet – just an earth closet which was emptied by the Dillyman. She cooked on a Primus stove and their only source of heating was a small fire. Washing had to be taken to her mother's in nearby Brian Avenue. The couple moved in in January and lived there for six months, after which they were re-housed in the huts which used to be at the top of Ings Lane – called Beverley Crescent.

Before the houses on Salisbury Avenue and Drive were built in the early 1950s, the land there was used for allotments and they stretched as far back as where Westfield Road is now. The Coops' father, Bill Coop, would borrow two heavy horses from Jack Chapman, who owned Grove Farm, and use them for ploughing and harrowing the land which was laid out in long, thin strips.

Cynthia Appleton, Derrick Coop and Christine Tindall

They were little tiny one-bedroom cottages

The new school was built in Manor Drive to replace the Church school and the Methodist school. When it was built I was eleven, so it would be 1957 or 1958. They wanted to use the windmill as the logo, the school badge. They called

Smedley Cottages, Manor Drive (date unknown). (North East Lincolnshire Council Libraries)

Smedley Cottages, Manor Drive, 2005. (North East Lincolnshire Council Libraries)

it the Leas School, I don't know why they used the name Leas, but they went to see my grandparents to see if they could do that and they said that was fine. When the school opened, my mother and grandma all went to the opening. I obviously went because I was going there to school, because they had closed the Church school and the Methodist school and I had a year to go before we did our Eleven Plus.

There is also [what] we called the Fishermen's cottages, and they were for fishermen when they retired. They were little tiny one-bedroom cottages, a row of them, six I think. I don't know when they were built; they were there as long as I can remember. Manor Drive, it came up opposite the church, straight and then it curved round. At the top of it they built the school and just to the side of the school was this row of cottages. Whether they were there before the school I can't remember. I think they had a name after an alderman or something. Then in the fullness of time they built more bungalows along there, and my mum and dad went in one of those.

Barbara West

The property boom

Taking a left turn at the end of Church Lane brings one into Skinners Lane. Much property development has taken place in the fields that once belonged to Church Farm. Heading in the direction towards Ings Lane and, on the right-hand side, stands the Tea Gardens. This has always been a popular venue for local folk from long before I was born. It was here that my eighth birthday party was held. I can well remember the occasion – the party music being played on an old portable windup gramophone borrowed from our neighbour and school friend, the late Malcolm Fytch.

The bungalow, built as a residence for Alec Archer the farmer, was not completed until about 1959. It was in the field on the opposite corner to Archer's bungalow that football practice took place. This period in time saw the beginning of further building development taking place in the lane. Facing the grounds of the Tea Gardens a row of bungalows were built, the end one of which (named High Winds) was the home of Peter Smith, painter and decorator. Peter and his apprentice, Roy Hallett, painted the exterior of my parents' house and that of our neighbour, the Bacons, every three years. Roy now has his own painting and decorating business and on the few occasions we meet he will always remind me of those distant times. The remaining fields were swallowed up, with the property boom of the last decade destroying the charm the Lane once held.

Peter Burns

Ings Lane

Taking a right turn from Skinners Lane by Archer's bungalow brings one into Ings Lane. On the left-hand side, beyond the cemetery, no development had taken place. Apart from the chicken farm (the diesel generator of which shattered the night air) and the remains of the air-raid shelters left over from the wartime airbase, there was not a thing to be seen – apart from the rabbits which were in abundance. Many finished in the pot having been dispatched by the Atkinson family who lived along with their neighbour Louis Vermeersch, the slaughter man, who resided at Tan Yard Farm. Walking one's dog down this lane at dusk, the generator would suddenly strike up, the sound of which would remind one of Lancaster aircraft engines and the many men who flew from the airbase never to return. One half expected to spot the ghostly apparition of a lost airman.

On the return journey only the Lodge to Grove House existed, and on its frontage a wind-powered generator, mounted on a pole, supplied electricity to a workshop used by the property owner who was an electrical engineer. Alternative technology is nothing new!

Grove House was divided into flats, the only occasion I visited this property being during my duties in later years as a Special Constable. By this time Grove House had become in a very run-down state. One duty was to check the derelict outbuildings for gangs of underage alcohol drinkers. This was an ongoing problem with youths not only from the village but from outside the area.

I will just finally mention that on the site where Camargue House now stands, a pond was located. This spot was covered with over-hanging trees and was a favourite place where as children we spent many hours pond dipping and acting out the adventures we had read about. Yes, truly they were happy days.

Peter Burns

🌸 Five 🌸

Shops and Businesses

The recollections in this chapter demonstrate one of the sharpest contrasts in our lives – the way in which our shopping habits have changed. Contributors describe a much slower way of life when shopping was much more of a social experience, giving people a chance to catch up on village news and gossip. There was none of the pressure and rush of trying to get through checkouts at supermarkets in record time so as not to hold up the next customer! Local shops are described with fond memories and conjure up images of polished display cabinets, glass doors and bow windows and, of course, the friendly shopkeeper who knew you and your family and had time to chat.

A lovely double-fronted shop

Topliss grocer's was a lovely double-fronted shop and when you opened the door you smelled everything when you walked in – on one side he sold clothes and material, cotton, elastic, all those sorts of things; on the other side it was food. He used to weigh all the sugar up in little bags, blue and purple, half a pound of sugar or a pound and it was all weighed up and then folded up. He used to have another shop that was at the other end of the High Street on the corner. He called it 'the branch'. It sold buckets and brushes and that sort of thing. He was a dapper little man, Sidney Topliss. He wore a pin-stripe suit with an old-fashioned collar and a bowler hat, always, and he always raised his hat to you and he always called you Mrs or Miss – Miss Stamford when he saw me – and raised his hat.

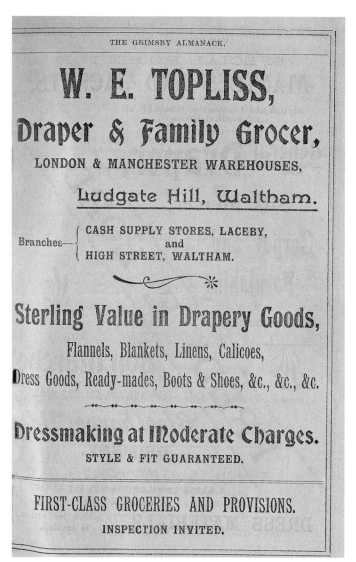

THE GRIMSBY ALMANACK.

W. E. TOPLISS,

Draper & Family Grocer,

LONDON & MANCHESTER WAREHOUSES,

Ludgate Hill, Waltham.

Branches— { CASH SUPPLY STORES, LACEBY,
and
HIGH STREET, WALTHAM.

Sterling Value in Drapery Goods,

Flannels, Blankets, Linens, Calicoes,

Dress Goods, Ready-mades, Boots & Shoes, &c., &c., &c.

Dressmaking at Moderate Charges.

STYLE & FIT GUARANTEED.

FIRST-CLASS GROCERIES AND PROVISIONS.

INSPECTION INVITED.

Extract from The Grimsby Almanack *(1898) showing an advertisement for Topliss shop. (North East Lincolnshire Council Libraries)*

Heather worked there in the '60s after school. I worked at Adams', which was on the other side of the High Street, and on a Saturday afternoon, 4 o'clockish probably, he'd say to Heather, 'I want you to go to the branch to collect the takings', and he timed her. He knew exactly how long it took to walk down the High Street, collect it and go back, and I would be at Adams' and we'd perhaps be going to the pictures or something at night, so I'd have to stand at the door to see her come back and shout, 'what time?', as she daren't stop, she had to keep walking, so she'd say, '7 o'clock for the bus,' 'ok then, see you later' and off she'd go. If I remembered something I'd have to wait for her coming back to tell her. Because he knew exactly to the second how long it took. You don't chat about either when you go to the branch, you go and you come straight back.

It was a lovely little shop. He lived down New Road where we lived. He lived at the other end in a bigger, nice house called the Laurels. He never got married; he had a lady friend and he had a car, I think it was a model T Ford. I believe it was in that car that he had an accident and died. The thing is, I never ever saw him go above 20 miles an hour, ever. But he was the last of the line of that family, which was an awful shame, because after him nobody wanted the shop because by then it was the 1960s and eventually it was pulled down. It was like an Edwardian shop and if you were a bit better off he had a chair, and if it was Mrs so and so, she would sit on the chair, while he ran about and got everything she wanted and brought it to her.

Barbara West

Worldly and impressive

There were two Topliss shops in the village. One stood opposite the library where the Co-op now stands and the other was at the end of the High Street. The latter was known as the 'top shop' and was referred to as 'our branch' by Mr Topliss. The top shop was run by a Miss Bailey. Other employees who worked in the shops were Miss Patchett and John Jacklin, who was the delivery man. The Topliss shop which stood opposite the library had a large yard and outbuildings to the rear. The wall which still stands today separated the land from Waltham Old Hall.

There was a large sign which hung outside the shop over the doorway – 'W.E. Topliss & Son, Grocers, Drapers est. 18? London and Manchester Warehouses'. To a child who had been brought up in a predominantly agricultural village, this was very worldly and impressive. Mr Topliss lived at No. 7 New Road.

A traveller (we would now call them reps) by the name of Mr Horran was a familiar visitor to the village shops. He was the Heinz rep and wore a bowler hat. He regularly visited the Topliss shops. Another rep was Mr Garrs – he was the rep for Marshalls Mill and was very polite.

Bill Adams

Miss Patchett, would you please get a chair for Mrs Wood

My mother placed a weekly grocery order with W.E. Topliss & Son Ltd in the village. On Fridays a Mr Burgin would come around in the morning from Topliss's and sit in the kitchen to write down in long-hand my mother's weekly

William Topliss outside his shop in the 1890s. (North East Lincolnshire Council Libraries)

food requirements. The next day (Saturday) the order would be delivered around lunch-time, either by van or by a special Topliss bicycle adapted to carry huge boxes full of groceries over a small front wheel. Usually John Jacklin either drove the van or rode the bicycle. He was a well-known Waltham character who was to stay with Mr Topliss until his shop closed. He then took a similar job with Tasker's butcher's shop at the end of High Street.

On rare occasions my mother would actually go into Topliss's main shop with its unique bow-fronted Victorian windows. Mr Topliss was a dapper, always smartly dressed, middle-aged man, who lived alone in a large house in New Road. It had been the home of his parents before they died. They are all buried in Waltham cemetery. Once into the shop Mr Topliss would call out for one of his female assistants to get a chair for my mother to sit on: 'Miss Patchett, would you please get a chair for Mrs Wood'. I recall the shop being very old-fashioned. Mr Topliss also had another shop, known as his 'Top Shop' that was on the corner of High Street and Barnoldby Road. The two shops were linked by phone – quite unusual then. If something wasn't available in one shop staff would ring the other in case it was available there.

Tom Wood

An embarrassing moment

On the opposite side of the road stood the shop of Mr Topliss, a gem of a building with its Georgian bow windows. Mr Topliss was a real gentleman, his catchphrase being 'are you being served madam?' This was his main shop where he sold groceries and haberdashery.

It was in this shop that I had an embarrassing moment as a young lad. My mother always bought my school shirts from this shop and it was on my way with my mother to buy some new ones that I was stung up the trousers by a wasp (in those days all schoolboys wore short trousers). She dragged me into the shop and in front of the young female assistant, Bessie Tharatt, pulled down my trousers so that one of the girls could apply a bag of Reckitt's Blue to the sting. This was an old remedy for wasp stings in those days. I was more concerned about my trousers being down than the actual sting.

Next to the shop of Mr Topliss was Wallers the butcher's. This shop had wooden shutters and when they were opened the carcasses of meat became exposed to the elements, creating a haven for flies in the warm weather. The shop was well known for its lack of hygiene, but it had a regular supply of customers. At the rear of the premises was a slaughter house. Elderly residents of the village can recall that after a beast was slaughtered, the blood was hosed away and left to drain down the slope into Trail Poke Lane.

Peter Burns

Topliss shop in the 1960s. (North East Lincolnshire Council Libraries)

Wonderful warm iced buns

Topliss Top Shop was on Ludgate Hill opposite where the library is now. W.E. Topliss was known as Billy Wet! Miss Bessie Patchett was the assistant at the Top Shop and Miss Ward was the assistant at the shop at the end of the High Street. High Street was known as Front Street. Topliss shop had a large display cabinet with glass doors and the cabinet housed a large jar of mustard. On a visit to the shop with mother when I was about eight or nine, I opened the glass doors, took the jar of mustard out and dropped it. Mother had to pay for the mustard!

Before the Adams came to the village, the baker's on the High Street where the saddlery is now was owned by Lowis's. There was also a tiny bakery opposite where you could buy wonderful warm iced buns wrapped in a cloth for 1d. They smelt delicious. Markham's grocer's shop was where our bakery is now, next to the library. Mr Markham had three daughters – Lily, Ruby and Kathleen. Ruby did the grocery deliveries on her bike. Fish and chip shops were plentiful in the village in the 1920s and '30s. There was one in Kirkgate, one in Skinners Lane and one where the florist is now on the High Street.

Evelyn Hemmingfield

A passion for conservation

C.J. Porter Tools Ltd – the engineers based at Newton Works, off Church Lane, Waltham – opened around 1954 and closed in 1990. It was a specialist company, a cornerstone of the British car industry, making precision tools and supplying a number of the country's leading manufacturers including Ford, British Leyland and Vauxhall. Kathleen Blyth was the company's clerical assistant and worked at Porter's for a total of thirty-six years.

Mr Cyril Porter was described as a wonderful man and was well liked among his staff. He had a passion for conservation and did not wish to impose the factory on the village itself. In fact, passers-by could be forgiven for not even noticing it was there. Staff could enjoy a cultivated lawn, flower-beds and fruit trees that surrounded the site – the factory itself was built on Waltham vicarage orchard.

Cyril Porter died in 1956 and his son Jim took over the business. Jim retired in 1990 and the factory was sold to a company called Dayson's, but it closed shortly afterwards after going into receivership. Ashlea Court Residential and Nursing Home now stands on the site.

Information sourced from the *Grimsby Evening Telegraph* Special Publication
(*Bygones* no. 108) Saturday 11 September 1999, pp 20-21

An aerial view of C.J. Porter Tools Ltd engineering works. (Courtesy of Mrs K. Blyth)

C.J. Porter Tools Ltd, site of engineering works. (Courtesy of Mrs K. Blyth)

CONTRACT OF EMPLOYMENT ACT, 1963
STATEMENT OF MAIN TERMS AND CONDITIONS OF EMPLOYMENT

NAME OF EMPLOYER	C.J. Porter Tools Ltd.,
NAME OF EMPLOYEE	BLYTH. Kathleen
DATE STATEMENT PREPARED	14 SEP 1964

(Note: If employment began five years or more ago, it is sufficient to say so.)
DATE EMPLOYMENT BEGAN 1st. May 1955

PAY

WAGE OR SALARY WILL BE PAID AT THE RATE OF £8.10.0d. PER (*) week
(* Insert interval of payment, i.e. per week or month etc.)

DETAILS OF OVERTIME PAY, PIECE-RATES ETC., IF APPLICABLE No overtime pay. Any bonuses paid are ex gratia and do not come within the scope of this agreement..

HOLIDAY ENTITLEMENT AND PAY

INCLUDE TERMS RELATING TO BANK HOLIDAYS & OTHER CUSTOMARY HOLIDAYS
As shown on the notice board.

SICKNESS OR INJURY

DETAILS OF TERMS AND CONDITIONS, AND ANY SICK PAY BENEFITS £8.10.0d., per week for 4 weeks.
A medical certificate is required if absent for three or more consecutive days.

PENSIONS AND PENSION SCHEMES

SCHEMES IN OPERATION – IF ANY, GIVE TERMS AND CONDITIONS The Company operates a non-contributory pension and life assurance scheme. Details are on the notice board.

NORMAL HOURS OF WORK

MON.	9 am.	TO 5.30 pm.
TUE.	9 am.	TO 5.30 pm.
WED.	9 am.	TO 5.30 pm.
THU.	9 am.	TO 5.30 pm.
FRI.	9 am.	TO 5.30 pm.
SAT.	9 am.	TO 12.0 noon
SUN.		TO

OTHER TERMS AND CONDITIONS – OVERTIME, PUNCTUALITY, MEAL BREAKS ETC.
Mid-day meal break from 12 noon to 1.30 pm., or as may be arranged to suit particular circumstances.
XXXXXXXXXXXXXXXXXXXXXX

RIGHTS TO NOTICE

TERMINATION OF EMPLOYMENT

AN EMPLOYEE IS ENTITLED TO RECEIVE ONE WEEKS NOTICE AFTER SIX MONTHS CONTINUOUS SERVICE, TWO WEEKS AFTER TWO YEARS CONTINUOUS SERVICE, AND FOUR WEEKS AFTER FIVE YEARS CONTINUOUS SERVICE. AN EMPLOYEE IS REQUIRED TO GIVE AT LEAST ONE WEEKS NOTICE. BY MUTUAL ARRANGEMENT, THESE NOTICES CAN BE WAIVED BY EITHER PARTY. PAYMENT IN LIEU OF NOTICE MAY BE GIVEN.

FIXED CONTRACTS

IF SERVICE IS BY FIXED CONTRACT, STATE EXPIRY DATE NONE.

OTHER INFORMATION

NOTE : – Where there are no particulars to be recorded under any of the headings – STATE 'NONE'

ANY CHANGES OF TERMS MENTIONED ABOVE WILL BE NOTIFIED, AND THE OFFICE RECORD IS AVAILABLE FOR INSPECTION.

© COPYRIGHT, 1964 PERCY JONES (*Fernbook*) LTD.

To re-order quote Ref. 1½ C.E.A

C.J. Porter Tools Ltd's contract of employment for Kathleen Blyth. (Courtesy of Mrs K. Blyth)

So off I went for the day, delivering meat

Next door, that was the butcher's, it had like a stable door. I never really remember going in there, but I assume my mother must have done. They also had a van, and he used to come round the houses even though it wasn't very far, selling out of the back of the van. I used to go with him sometimes, because he used to go round all the villages, Tetney, Fulstow and what have you. Because my brother used to go with my grandad on the lorry delivering flour and corn and stuff, one day the butcher came to deliver to my mother and me, and I had got a monk on because I couldn't go out, and he said what's the matter, and I said that I wanted to go [on the Mill delivery], they'd gone round villages, Binbrook, all that way. He said, well you can come with me if you want. So my mum said ok, it was alright, so off I went for the day, delivering meat. I did that a few times.

There were two brothers that ran it [the butcher's]: John and Cyril. It was Cyril that used to do the deliveries; John was mostly in the shop. His daughter still lives in the village, Shirley, they call her. I think she's the same age as my older brother, I think they were at school together. That was the thing: a lot of us had brothers perhaps ten years older because of the war. So a lot of us were like two tier families.

When that closed [the butcher's], they decided, because Topliss' was empty and the house was already empty next door to it, it had gone a bit to wrack and ruin. So they decided to pull them all down, so Wallers moved, they had a little lock up, it's still there, just a little square shop round in the top of Fairway. I think Cyril died fairly young as far as I can remember, but John Waller ran the other one on his own until he retired from that, but delivered in the village until well into his eighties.

I always remember the butcher's had like a wooden stable door and it was painted red. Not in my time that I can remember, but they used to slaughter the animals as well, when my mother was younger, and the blood used to run down into the drain or down the road. I always walked on the other side of the road because it always felt a bit creepy to me.

On the other side of the road was a rectory. There was a really high wall around it, and of course you know what children are like. They reckoned that it was haunted. My brother used to deliver the papers then and his friend used to go with him, and he used to open the gate and run, put the paper through and run back again, then his friend shut the gate. There is nothing of the rectory left now.

Later on, when I was at school, I worked there [the butcher's] after school for my pocket money, from 4 o'clock to 6 o'clock and all day on a Saturday. Lots of us did out of the village, as one left another one went, but I stayed until I was sixteen. Then I went into Grimsby to work.

Barbara West

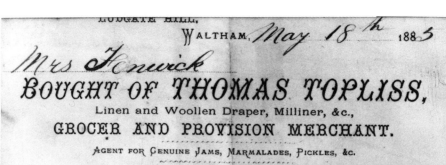

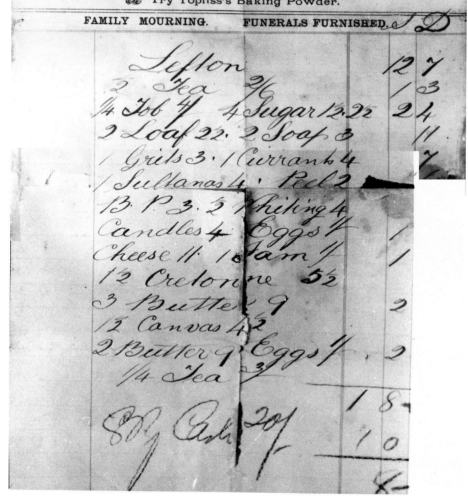

Topliss shop bill, 1885. (North East Lincolnshire Council Libraries)

Telephone : WALTHAM 3147.

HIGH STREET,

WALTHAM,......*June 16*......19*50*

1911

Mrs Asquith

Bought of **S. R. ADAMS,**

GROCER, BAKER & CONFECTIONER

4 lbs 13oz Wedding Cake @ 3/4 lb   £2-4-4

1 Ornament } on 4 Pillars } Loan   5-0

£2-9-4

Paid Bath 16/6/50

Adams shop bill, 1950. (Courtesy of Mrs K. Blyth)

'Old man Harrison'

Waller's butchers pre-dated Taskers. Waller's was on the High Street situated between what is now Fairway and the Co-op. It was adjacent to Topliss shop and had its own slaughter house in Trail Poke Lane.

Harrison's grocers and corn merchant's was run by 'old man Harrison'. He sold, amongst other things, chicken feed and cattle cake which was sold in planks and had to be cut up. Ludgate Close used to be Harrison's orchard.

There were two bakers in the village. The Adams had a baker's shop and there was also Lowis's. 'Flash ovens' were installed in one of the baker's. They would have a solid base and walls and tie rods. A perfect brick arch was above the solid base. Sand etc. was placed on top of the oven to insulate it. Fire was made in the fire box and when the coals were red hot they were thrown in the oven to heat it up. The coals were then raked out and the oven was flailed. The flail was a pole with a chain on the end and a wet sack was attached to the chain. The purpose of the flailing was to remove soot from the oven and to create steam.

Harry Jackson was the village blacksmith. A little-known fact is that he was left-handed. You might notice that the point of the anvil which is now on the village green is set to the left.

Bill and Ray Adams

A roaring trade

Trail Poke Lane was where the entrance to Fairway is located. The only dwellings at that time were the houses in Mount Pleasant, the lane then leading to a farm. At the junction of the land and the High Street stands Cobblers Cottage, now renovated and renamed Lilac Cottage; this is the oldest dwelling in the village. This property has seen many tenants over the centuries, once used as a baker's and later a cobbler's, it was part of a group of cottages that extended to where the present post office and chemist shop stands. These cottages had pigsties in their gardens. Buck Beck used to flow past the end of the cottage. It was an open drain passing under the road, and ran through into Kirkgate.

The flower shop was then a fish and chip shop owned by the Rickall family. It was very popular and did a roaring trade with the airmen from RAF Grimsby. Fish and chips being a staple diet in the 1950s with local Grimsby fish in abundance.

On the opposite side of the road stood the original King's Head public house, built forward of where the new one now stands. Mrs Mountain the licensee held sway, but it was knocked down before I was the legal age to partake of Hewitts beer, Hewitts being the Grimsby brewers who owned the premises. Adjacent to the pub was the original post office where Mrs Kendall was the

King's Head public house in the early 1900s. (North East Lincolnshire Council Libraries)

High Street with former fire station, 1968. (North East Lincolnshire Council Libraries)

post mistress. Her son Jack was the postman and he would often mutter at you as he passed by on his bike. Next door was Mrs Greaves' wool shop. It was from here that my father used to fetch home a parcel every month for my mother. It was always wrapped in brown paper and [when I] asked what it contained, I was told to mind my own business. Those were innocent days before sex education was taught in schools.

The post office was later converted into another chippy and was destroyed along with the wool shop in a fire. Mrs Ballans took over the wool shop when Mrs Greaves retired and after the fire the business was transferred to a shop across the road. Before Mrs Ballans took over the premises it was used as a DIY shop by Mr Belk the local builder. This property has now been converted into a cottage.

Crossing the road again and passing the restaurant (Shires), we come to an eight foot adjacent to the saddler's shop. In those days it was owned by the Adams family and was a grocer's. Up the eight foot was the garage of Spencer & Vance Motor Engineers and in the yard was a hand-cranked petrol pump dispensing FINA petrol. It was to this garage that my father would take the hire car for petrol before going on our holidays. Peter Spence, who co-owned the garage, was an aircraft engineer maintaining the Lancaster bombers that flew from Waltham aerodrome during the war. His partner in the business was Mr Vance, an electrical engineer. The little shop across the road that was lately a boutique was owned by him and was the local cycle shop run by his wife.

The large shop next to this was built by the Adams family when they enlarged their grocery business. This was taken over by the Co-operative Group and has seen various types of business use since then. Passing Pretoria House and its adjacent cottage, the flooring shop was originally two cottages before being converted by Mr Belk into yet another DIY store. I worked for the builder at the time of the conversion and the remains of a bake house were discovered; however, this was not surprising as in the yard behind the property stood the original Waltham mill which was a post mill demolished before the tower mill was built on Brigsley Road.

Adjacent to the tile shop stands the old fire station, the doors of which are now painted dark blue. On the roof of the building was mounted the air-raid siren, which was tested long after the war was over. We older residents can still remember the 'all clear' being sounded once a month. Next to the old fire station and now the barber's shop was the other shop of Mr Topliss. Here he sold linoleum and coconut matting along with hardware.

Looking across the road a little back up the High Street you will see the dilapidated shop of Taskers, a premier butcher's in its heyday, owned by Thomas Tasker who was a farmer. It was very popular and hygienic and you always received a friendly and first-class service from Robby, Tom's son, backed by Harold Donnington who lived in the cottage next to the shop and Maurice his assistant.

Peter Burns

A favourite stopping off place

I always thought it rather odd in those immediate post-war days that there were so many grocers' shops in what was then not the biggest of villages. Other than the two Topliss shops, there was Cater's in Kirkgate (which also had an off-licence) on the same spot as the Spar shop today. Then Harrison's on the corner of High Street, where it joins Kirkgate – the shop is still there – and, of course, Adams' at the far end of High Street, on the same side as Tasker's butchers shop. There was also Waller's butchers shop just around the corner from Topliss's in Fairway. Also in High Street was the old post office, which rather strangely also sold clothes. I cannot recall the family which ran it, but the son (was it Jack, or John?) occasionally delivered the afternoon post. He would open the front door of the house (no need to live behind locked doors in those days) and hurl the post into the house and loudly shout to remind you that it was there.

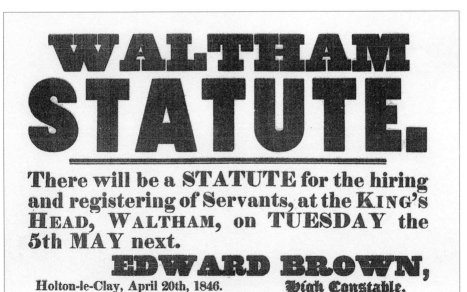

Notice for Waltham Statute, 1846. (Skelton Collection, North East Lincolnshire Council Libraries)

High Street was also the site of the original King's Head public house. It was a very much smaller pub than its much larger well-known namesake is today. It was mainly run by the Mountain family, although around this time I think the Williamsons may have taken it over. It was a favourite stopping off place of my father's for a 'quick one' on his way home from 'down dock'. Nearly opposite the old pub was the fish and chip shop, which did a roaring trade when it was open. There were a number of smaller shops and terraced houses, named Providence Buildings, in High Street too. Often outside one, in a wheelchair, was a young lady whose name eludes me now. She always gave you a smile when you passed her by or stopped for a chat. In those days Waltham also had a police station, near the end of Brigsley Road in a partially converted office/house. The local 'bobby' there kept a tight control of events and made sure there were no crime waves.

Tom Wood

Did someone ring?

In the 1940s and '50s Ern Fowler delivered the coal. Mr Palmer was the fish merchant and had a blue van and milk would be delivered in churns by Sid Brumpton and old man Grantham. The Archers had a milk pasteurising business. You could buy pink and white sugar mice from Cater's store.

The Topliss shop opposite the library had a preservation order on it but unfortunately it was burnt down.

For people who shopped at Harrison's (the car part shop now) an added bonus was getting hold of the empty orange boxes. They could be turned on their sides and used as bedside cabinets. Mother paid 6d or 1s for one. Oranges would come individually wrapped in tissue paper and the paper was also useful as loo paper, much better than the usual newspaper that was used!

Mr Beeley the barber was at the end of New Road just before the Methodist school. Girls would go there too to get their hair cut.

Something called a premium stallion scheme was run from the King's Head and was designed to upgrade local stock.

The 'snug' in the pub was just that – snug! Full of smoke and rather dark. Mrs Drummond, who worked behind the bar, would come out when customers rang the bell saying, 'Did someone ring?'

Cynthia Appleton, Derrick Coop and Christine Tindall

Gob stoppers, liquorice sticks and penny chews

A left turn at the junction of New Road with the High Street brings us into Kirkgate. The motor spares shop was originally Harrison's the grocers and it was here that I used to go shopping for sugar and tea for my mother, who liked to patronise various shops in the village with regard to grocery purchases. Sugar used to be packed in blue paper bags and the packets of PG Tips loose tea contained tea cards. As I collected these cards I did not mind going to the shop for them.

Next to Harrison's stood Percy Cater's general store and when one entered the premises the wonderful aroma associated with village stores greeted you, the smells ranging from apples to paraffin. Percy Cater had a daughter named Mary who taught at All Saints' Church Sunday School. Mary was very pretty and a lovely teacher, so I had no objections to attending lessons on a Sunday morning. Sadly Mary has long since passed away and the shop was demolished to make way for Tates Store (now Spar). In the group of cottages next to Cater's shop lived Roy Green at No. 3. John Rushby lived at No. 5 and Alice Scott at No. 7. The detached house separated from the cottages by Well Lane was the residence of Rose Day although I recollect a connection with Bill Buffam who used to play the trumpet, the sound of which could be heard as one passed by.

The next property in the row was the fish and chip shop and I remember fish and chips being priced at 1s 3d including scraps. This building was, at a later date, used as a workshop by the joiner Steve Sawycky. Next to these premises the open Beck flowed, the public house being protected by a parapet wall beyond which stood a fine old Georgian house that formed part of the row. I remember attending the auction of the house contents before its demolition. The Beck now flows beneath a culvert and a new dwelling has been built on the site of these properties.

Fortunately, the other old cottages in this row survive as does the villa 'Windsor', the former home of John Fowler and now renamed 'Kirklees'. It was next to this property that the Church of England school was located, new bungalows being erected on the site after the school was demolished. On the opposite side of Kirkgate, and before the widening of the junction with Cheapside, stood Danesbury House, the home of the Blakeman family. A pair of semi-detached houses now stand near its former location. Beyond the entrance to Kirkside stands a row of terrace houses, of which some residents I can recall during the late 1950s – Arthur Watson, William Wright, Robert Burkitt and George Scoffin spring to mind. At the end of the terrace the open Beck flowed from beneath the High Street.

By the side of the Beck the premises which now contain the hairdresser's was formerly the second DIY shop owned by Eddie Belk the builder, the adjacent premises, which is now the opticians, I seem to recall was used by a cobbler. A large

The Tilted Barrel. (By Christopher Midgley, Leas Junior School)

wooden building stood in the yard at the rear and was used as a timber store for the DIY shop. In later years it was used as a joiner's workshop by Steve Sawycky before his move into the old fish and chip shop. The Tilted Barrel public house was a private residence before its conversion by John Snape the builder. I can vaguely remember an old thatched cottage standing near to where the present car park entrance is located. The premises which are now the Tea Room and Tanning Studio were formerly a cottage; however, I cannot recall the name of the resident. On the corner of Kirkgate and facing the High Street the baker's shop was, back in my childhood days, Greens Sweet Shop. It was from here that you purchased gob stoppers, liquorice sticks and penny chews.

Peter Burns

❧ Six ❧

Waltham Windmill

Waltham Windmill is a well-known landmark in the village. The present mill was built in the late 1880s after the post mill occupying the site was blown down in 1873. The mill was a working mill within living memory and there are delightful reminiscences of one member of the milling family included in this chapter.

Nowadays the windmill site attracts many visitors, who can enjoy the historical surroundings and museum as well as the many small businesses, car boot sales and miniature railway rides that take place there.

Uncle Tom and Bill used to paint the outside with tar

There are two things about the sails, I don't know whether a barrage balloon brought one off, but I remember my grandma telling me about one coming off in a gale and landing outside the parlour window. Maybe they had one that could have been replaced but when the other one came off they couldn't replace two and it has been four as long as I can remember. My brother (Bill Stamford), he used to work at the mill. He did National Service, obviously, and in between time he worked at the mill and Uncle Tom and Bill used to paint the outside with tar, in like a cradle, started at the top and it was let down slowly, and it used to take all the summer, near enough. They used to paint the top with a white liquid that Uncle Tom used to make up, and it was linseed oil, lime, and something pretty lethal, I can't remember what it was. In these days you just wouldn't get away with it and he mixed it all in a big barrel and then they took it up in bucketfuls and painted it on the top and on the sails. Bill used to come out along the top and on the fan. I never went to the top; it always felt as though it was moving to me. In the mill there were wooden doors dividing each floor and there was a big chain went through from the sails right down to the bottom. They used to store the grain at the top of the mill originally, and they used to grind it and put it into the sacks, fasten it up, fasten it to this chain, and the other chain was on a pulley thing, and the sack went up through all the doors and as it went the doors would shut, but we'd sit on them sometimes and go up.

Barbara West

They used to send the postcard in the morning

The postcards were used for orders for the mill, for flour or bran or whatever the farmers mostly wanted. They used to send the postcard in the morning, quite often, or the day before, because they [the mill] delivered twice a week as a rule and they had separate areas, so the farmer, wherever he was from, would know which area they were going to on a Tuesday and a Friday. Friday they went Binbrook way and all the villages between and Tuesday I think they went more towards Scunthorpe and that way round. They didn't go, as far as I know, to Scunthorpe, but being a girl I wasn't allowed to go anyway. My brother used to go.

Originally they were using a horse and cart, for quite a long time. Even after the war they had a pony and trap. My brother can remember them having a pony and trap until the mid 1940s, until after I was born. Billy, I don't know why they called the pony Billy.

I don't know how long they used them for, the postcards. I know that straight after the war they had a telephone. I don't know whether they had one before. So from then I expect they used the telephone, and if the farmers had a phone, or depending where the farms were, sometimes they went to a post office or a house that had a phone. But a lot of the farms were out in the wilds, particularly the ones out Binbrook way, like Walesby and Tealby and so on. They were only tiny villages.

They used to load up early on a Friday, and off they go and it would be nearly dark when they came back at night after delivering around the farms. Both grandad [George Rodgers] and Uncle Tom [Rodgers] went on the deliveries and Bill [Stamford] when he worked for them, and they did the grinding in between times, usually during the week, not often at the weekends, unless there had been no wind, because until the mid 1950s they used wind to drive the sails. Sometimes when there wasn't any for days or weeks during the summer, they

Waltham Windmill, c. 1905. (North East Lincolnshire Council Libraries)

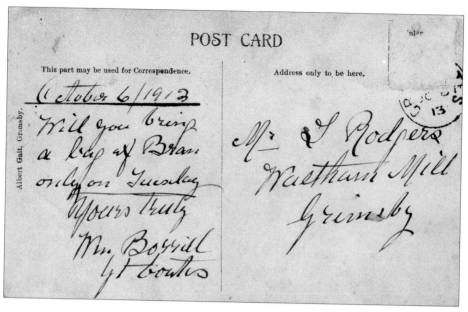

A postcard showing an order for a cup of bran, 1913. 'October 6th 1913. Will you bring a cup of bran only on Tuesday. Yours truly Mr Borrill, Gt Coates.' (Courtesy of Mrs B. West)

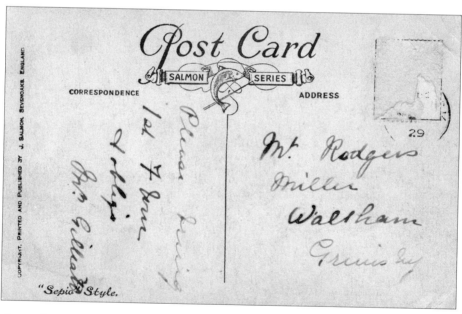

A postcard order for flour from Waltham Windmill, 1929. 'Please bring 1sh Flour. Oblige. Mr Gilliatt.' (Courtesy of Mrs B. West)

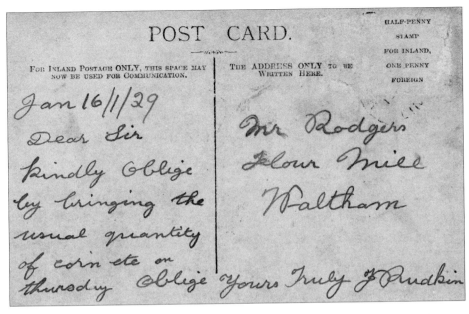

A postcard order for corn. 'January 16th 1929. Dear Sir, Kindly oblige by bringing the usual quantity of corn etc on Thursday. Oblige yours truly J Rudkin.' (Courtesy of Mrs B. West)

would mill during the night. Grandad, a tiny bit of wind and his ear would be up and he'd be up and off, so sometimes they would mill all night, until four or five o'clock in the morning.

Barbara West

A scene from a war film

The windmill in my younger days was owned by the Rodgers family. The mill was powered by an auxiliary engine. The old railway coach which is now a tea room was used as accommodation and the wartime buildings which were used by the WAAF and the Home Guard resembled a scene from a war film. It's thanks to the late Frank Dunham and the handful of enthusiasts, including myself, who founded the Preservation Society that the mill still exists today.

Frank Dunham lived in the bungalow facing the mill, after formerly residing in the High Street, and was a foreman at Ogles Timber Mill at New Waltham. He was a great character from an old Waltham family who spoke with a true Lincolnshire dialect. Some of his phrases still come to mind.

Peter Burns

Waltham Windmill, c. 1870. (North East Lincolnshire Council Libraries)

Everybody was soaking wet up to the knees

When war first broke out and they where having bombing raids, they used to go in the mill, because the mill was a landmark so they thought it was perfectly safe. But then there was some to-do over wanting to pull the mill down because it was a landmark for the Germans, so while they were deciding that, my grandparents decided to build a kind of a shelter in the ditch. Half way down it was – ever so deep – and they put all the stuff in and when the next raid came they all went and sat in there. So they did this a time or two, and then it rained and everything and everybody was soaking wet up to the knees, so they never used it any more. Grandma wasn't having it, so it was back in the mill or stay in bed! So they decided to stay in their beds.

In the meantime they got a map from the RAF at Waltham showing the landmarks that they used and the mill was one of them, so they said there was no way they would let anyone pull it down because, whether the Germans used it or not, they used that landmark and they gave them the map so that they wouldn't pull it down.

Barbara West

Grandad used to mill during the night if the wind was right

They used the mill as a lookout, the Home Guard during the war. Grandad [George Rodgers] got hauled off to jail once, because the mill was up on a hill and the main house then faced the village, and of course there was a black-out and everything. Also then there was just the one village bobby who lived in a house down Front Street. The jail was just sort of a room in his house. I suppose it had bars on it; I don't know. Grandad used to mill during the night if the wind was right, he'd do the milling whenever the wind was right, not necessarily during the day. So him and my uncle were in and out of the mill. Grandad was a law unto himself really and he was just in and out and he didn't care. Well lo and behold before morning came, up came the policeman to haul him off for signalling to the enemy out at sea because the door kept opening and closing and the light kept showing, so they took him down to the jail until they got it all sorted out.

In 1940 or 1941 the Irish navvies came to build a WAAF camp up there. When they were building it, my brother at the time was about five and he has always been into everything. So he used to go across and they used to give him little jobs to do. 'Billy come and do this, Billy come and do that.' On a Friday they paid him and they had a little box thing where a man sat with the money in envelopes and when the navvies came along to be paid; they brought him along and one of them used to bring a box and put it down and say 'up on the box Billy, get your pay', and he used to get a penny or tuppence in an envelope.

Waltham Windmill. (By Maddie Fox, Leas Junior School)

Waltham post mill on the site of the current windmill, c. 1865. (North East Lincolnshire Council Libraries)

The downside was that Irish navvies tend to swear a little bit. So, he could swear like a trooper and so my mother was a little worried about where she would take him. Because in the village she used to go to whist drives once a week, of course they were all old ladies, because there no men, much, because it was war time and he would say some not very nice things and she'd have to haul him out or gag him!

Ross Hall, as it was called then, there's a stage thing and when they play whist they move round and a lot of them used to take their children, but there was a stage and Billy was up on the stage one day after being moved round and a lady sat there in front of him, so he bent down and he looked at her and he said, 'now, you old b★★★★r', patting her on the side of the face. So my mother was not really impressed with that, so she took him home quickly.

Barbara West

Village Memories

In Waltham village I was born,
Early one August morn.
England's victory still in mind
The horrors of war put behind.

Memories of Waltham I still have,
Some are happy, but many sad.
Schooldays remembered with some
Regret and of times I would rather forget.

Life moves on and friends have gone
Forever some I fear, but I am still here
To recall some of my memories
Not all.

I have rallied the Cubs and pounded the Beat
Dealt with trouble on the village street.
Left my mark in ink and paint of when the time
The village was quaint.

On land and sea I have travelled far
By aircraft, ship and motorcar.
From Canada's Rocky Mountains,
To Australia's sandy shores
And given half a chance,
I will sail the seas some more.

So when my time comes to cross the Bar,
No need to take me very far.
Just down Ings Lane and let me lay,
Amongst the local folk I pray.
It matters not for where I roam
Let Waltham always, be my home.

Peter J. Burns, February 2009

Other titles published by The History Press

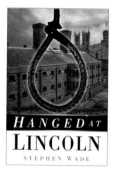

Hanged at Lincoln
STEPHEN WADE

Hanged at Lincoln gathers together the stories of criminals hanged at both Lincoln Castle Prison and HMP Lincoln on Greetwell Road between 1716 and 1961. The condemned featured here range from coiners and forgers to thieves, highwaymen and poisoners. Among the infamous murderers executed at Lincoln include Richard Insole, executed in 1887 for the murder of his wife; child-killer Frederick Nodder, hanged in 1937; and Herbert Leonard Mills, who failed to commit the perfect murder and was hanged in 1951 by Albert Pierrepoint.

978 0 7509 5110 4

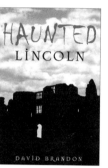

Haunted Lincoln
DAVID BRANDON

The half-timbered buildings that cling to the steep streets and narrow lanes of the city of Lincoln groan under the weight of thousands of years of history. Not surprisingly, this ancient city is rife with tales of spectral spirits and ghastly ghouls. Even the more workaday areas can boast haunted pubs, residences and mysterious goings-on in the theatre. In this book the area immediately around Lincoln itself is explored, with reports of dancing stones, roadside apparitions and omens of death in deserted churchyards.

978 0 7524 4891 6

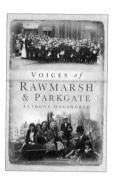

Voices of Rawmarsh & Parkgate
ANTHONY DODSWORTH

This book is the culmination of more than a year's research by the Rawmarsh and Parkgate Local History Group. Filled with stories that will move, remind and delight the reader, every aspect of life in the area is here. From memories of the Queen's Coronation and Second World War to schooldays and working lives – and, of course, some of Rawmarsh's famous characters – this nostalgic volume will delight all who know the area. It is an essential record of times that have now gone forever.

978 0 7524 4842 8

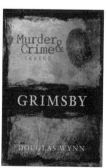

Murder & Crime: Grimsby
DOUGLAS WYNN

Retold for a new generation are shocking stories of infanticide, drunken brawls in town, the jealous, alcohol-fuelled raging of one betrayed husband, as well as the only instance in the town's recorded history when a cooking implement has been used as a lethal weapon. Mixing historical documents with contemporary photography, Douglas Wynn's collection of true crimes provides a mesmerising evocation of the past. It's sure to haunt the imagination of any reader with an interest in the history of the town and the surrounding area.

978 0 7524 4295 2

Visit our website and discover thousands of other History Press books.
www.thehistorypress.co.uk